WILLIAM TURNBULL

WILLIAM TURNBULL BEYOND TIME

WADDINGTON GALLERIES 2010

WILLIAM TURNBULL

ON SCULPTURE & PAINTING

The sculpture that I have liked is sculpture that is very simple … not ornate. Sculpture which has very simple shapes … early Greek sculpture, early Egyptian sculpture … different places where the shapes are fairly simple and the colouring is fairly simple … and the periods of sculpture which I have liked right from the earliest times have tended to be the opposite of baroque

It was very much at one point 'are you a painter or a sculptor?' I'd always done both and I never considered, much to certain people's annoyance, one more important than the other

I was very much concerned that a sculpture was an object and a painting was an object. The paintings I made were objects, they weren't illusions. They didn't refer to something else, they only refer to themselves, and so they were actually in the same area but they were made with different stuff

The main thing was emphasizing the painting as an object rather than a kind of visual experience

But it's not a painting of something … like a flower or a person or anything like that

I remember when I got hooked on these single colour paintings and couldn't figure out whether it was worth spoiling them by putting another colour on it

It's amazing how powerful colour is

ON FLYING

When you're flying a plane and looking down at a landscape it's nothing like the same landscape as the one Constable was painting

Suddenly you looked down and there was just endless abstraction … it was a new way of seeing the world. It certainly made me have a totally different attitude as to what was visually 'the reality'

And one of the things I remember coming into my head quite a lot was the fact that, at different times, I was up there and there was nothing else. You had an idea of space and movement that you didn't get in a motor car … three-dimensional space and movement … and you just felt in the middle of nowhere. It was beautiful. You could just go up there, without anyone else, and fly around for an hour and come back to earth again

ON PARIS (1948–50)

I went there (Paris) because I wasn't very interested in the art scene in London or the artists in London and I was interested in the artists in Paris and what had been going on there for quite a long time

I think the most enjoyable time as far as art was concerned was in Paris. I got on very well with the people I met there. I liked the art, I always had done. I felt I was in the place I really belonged

But the artist I saw that was most important to me was Alberto Giacometti whose work made an enormous impression on me at that time … I met him and visited him on a number of occasions over the time I was in Paris

There were a lot of things that were interesting at the time, for me to meet artists like Braque and Brancusi and people like that. To actually see the person and see what the person was like apart from the work

I had a very strange experience at Brancusi's studio. I'd heard he wouldn't let you in unless you were somebody. I got there and he opened the door, and I put my foot in the door and he couldn't close it, and I just kept saying to him that I admired his work so much. It was difficult to see it anywhere else; there was none of it in the museums. Why couldn't he just let me in? And I've never forgotten this, he let me in and left the room. He had these beautiful covers over a lot of the sculptures, he took them off and walked out of the room and left me there. And he came back after about 15 or 20 minutes and said 'you have to go now'. Later, when I thought about it, I thought 'how did you ever have that kind of luck Turnbull?', for something like that to happen, but then he was one of the artists I admired the most and it was very difficult to see his work anywhere else

NEW YORK (FIRST VISIT IN 1957)

I began to make contact with the artists from New York and I liked enormously what I was seeing there. I think what was going on in New York at the time was quite extraordinary, quite different from anything else. It just seemed to happen quite suddenly

I had an introduction through (Donald) Blinken to quite a number of the American artists at that time and went to visit their studios. Rothko … people like that. I met all of them

There's certain artists whose work you just have an immediate enthusiasm for, like with Pollock and Rothko, Clyfford Still … people like that. I thought enormously highly of them. I was taken round by Blinken and they were still in their old studios. They were all in the places where they had painted all these pictures … they weren't rich. They were just starting to be able to make some money. So it was very interesting to go to New York and see what it had been like for a while rather than what it became

It is one of the few works of sculpture that I could honestly say would sit quietly and beautifully with our room of Rothkos. Because both the sculpture and the Rothkos require contemplation. They're not the sort of things that knock you over the first time you see them. You have to sit with them and look at them and listen to them speak to you and the Turnbull speaks of an approach to art which is both contemporary but also timeless. Also classic.

You must admit, she's lovely isn't she?
Ambassador Donald Blinken (talking about *Standing Female Figure*, 1956 by William Turnbull)

… once I started buying Rothko and Guston and Tworkov and de Kooning, most of the European things tended to disappear. Only the Turnbulls survived and some Giacometti drawings, because those are the works I think are timeless and complement the New York School
Ambassador Donald Blinken

The important thing is that, once I introduced Bill to one of the New York artists, he didn't need me after that to continue the relationship. Once he met them, he was part of the group and he got along very, very well. So if he met Rothko through me or he met Jack Tworkov through me, for example, that was it. After that, Bill could carry on his own correspondence with them or visit their studios or invite them to see him when they were in London. It was a very happy and easy time for me and for him
Ambassador Donald Blinken

He does not suffer fools gladly, but more importantly, he is not willing to compromise either his own work, or the relationships he has with museums or dealers. That's the way he is. He can't change that. I think the benefit of that is that his work has always been clear and direct and is clearly his own and nobody else's
Ambassador Donald Blinken

He was also in a way of course probably exemplary in the sense of being a 'Modernist' although when you were in the middle of it we didn't know what 'Modernism' was then
Tess Jaray

There was a big difference between Bill in the early days when I knew him, and after he married Kim. I think Kim opened so many doors for him and made him so happy that I think it made a great deal of difference to his work because I think probably his heart was given freer rein
Tess Jaray

I think Bill's relation to the Modern and the Modern Movement … he was certainly part of that and emerged from it but he always seemed to me to have a vision and a cultural connection that went back centuries … millennia even. There's something ancient as well as modern about a lot of his work. And also there's a 'timelessness'
Tim Marlow

I owned a couple of Matisse découpés … and I saw in Bill's work the same thing I saw in Rothko and Gottlieb and Matisse … once you got back behind the early works … it's essentially about colour
Lord McAlpine of West Green

Bill can draw. He gave me a present of about six drawings done in the style of a great Japanese printmaker … absolutely fantastic. Beautifully drawn. A quality of drawing you very seldom see. And I don't think people think about Bill for drawings. But these drawings are sensational. Very beautiful
Lord McAlpine of West Green

There is a great subtlety about his work that isn't immediately apparent. A lot of it looks large, tough, straightforward. But it's far from being straightforward. It's much, much deeper. And certainly, in my view, it's based on the reaction of the person to the painting, rather than the painting carrying a message … it's not like a picture of haystacks or apples … it's a blank canvas which can reflect your whole life or just a bit of it
Lord McAlpine of West Green

A lot of the others … they're good, some were very clever but they kind of get a bit flaky. I've never seen a flaky Turnbull. They're all absolutely right there
Lord McAlpine of West Green

The remarkable thing about Bill is the way in which he has
stayed true to his own values, spirit and intellectual
position over a fifty, sixty year period
Sir Nicholas Serota

Here's a young man whose been in the RAF, who goes to
Paris and ends up at the age of less than 30 making a body
of work that can stand comparison with Giacometti and
other mature artists working in the 40s and 50s. Of course
he was aware of their work and he was influenced by what
they were doing, but it is a very distinct body of work
Sir Nicholas Serota

The way in which he was working at that moment was
obviously significant and had a profound influence on
other artists in Britain … Bill's thinking informed ideas
about sculpture and also ideas that ultimately led to
The Independent Group
Sir Nicholas Serota

It's interesting that his work was very much appreciated
in America in the early 60s. He showed at Malborough-
Gerson. The works were bought in America … and if you
talk to an artist like Carl Andre he was very aware of what
Bill was doing. I remember asking Carl 'who are the British
artists who you admire and respect?' and … immediately
the name Turnbull came out.

I think Bill's significance in America is probably much
greater than has previously been recognized. At least
among the artists
Sir Nicholas Serota

I happen to see a very clear connection between the
paintings and the sculpture. It's particularly interesting
if you see the sculpture alongside the paintings. Again if
you look at the patina on the sculpture and the way he
rather innovatively uses colour to bring out the qualities
in the sculpture and even plays with different patinas for
the same cast.

The delicacy of the brushstrokes, the subtlety of the works
… the spontaneity that you see in the paintings, the energy
… is something you will see in the surface of the sculpture
as well
Michael Uva

I forget which day Bill taught life drawing. I'd just sneak in the back and listen to him. He was marvellous. He drew at the same time as he taught … it was incredible, like a happening. I'd just sit back there and wonder. Barry (Flanagan) would do the same. He was a magnificent teacher … a pedagogue, in the real sense of the word
Brian Wall

He has an unrelenting mind. A great unrelenting mind. He has a mind that goes into the problem. It goes round the problem. It goes over the problem. It destroys the problem
Brian Wall

In the end it's about what you have to say and not to half say what someone else has. And the great thing about Turnbull is that's what he was. Come what may it doesn't matter what happens, this is the way it's going to be. He's going to carve his own path … to wherever it was going to lead him
Brian Wall

THE WORKS

1

Mask
1946
bronze
cast no.4 from an edition of 4 plus 1 artist's cast
15 ½ × 9 ¼ × ⅝ in / 39·4 × 23·5 × 1·6 cm
on York stone base

2

Heavy Insect
1949
bronze
cast no.4 from an edition of 4 plus 1 artist's cast
20 ½ × 33 ¼ × 8 ¾ in / 52 × 84·5 × 22·2 cm

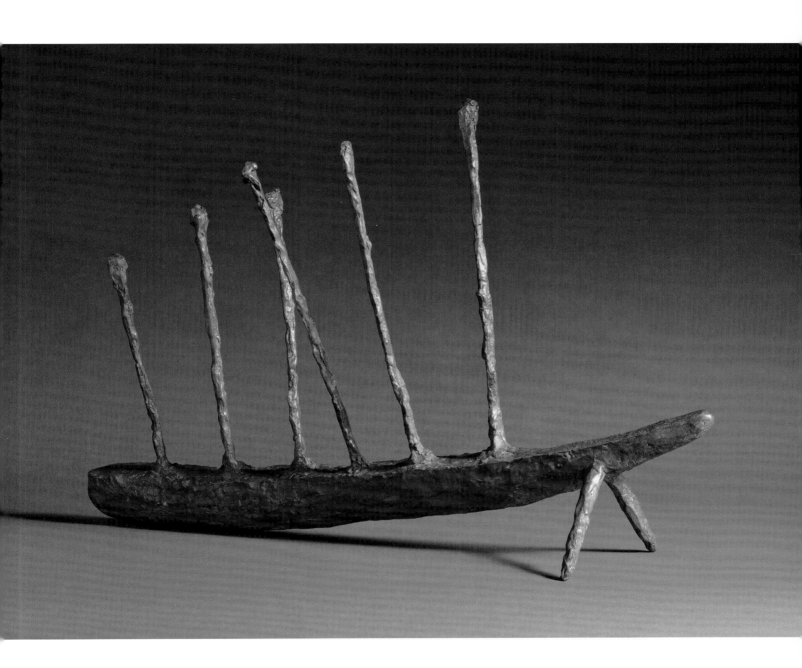

3

Hanging Sculpture
1949
plaster over wire (to be cast in a bronze edition of 6 plus 1 artist's cast)
48 in / 121·9 cm wide

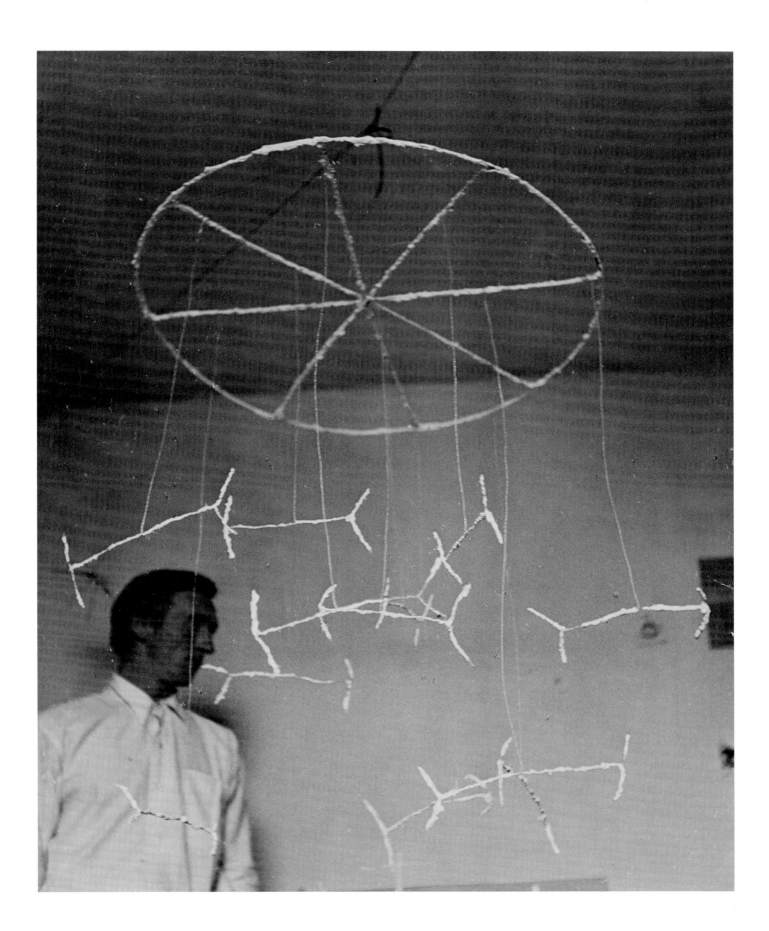

4

Forms on a Base
1949
bronze, unique
13 ¼ × 13 ½ × 18 ½ in / 33·7 × 34·3 × 47 cm

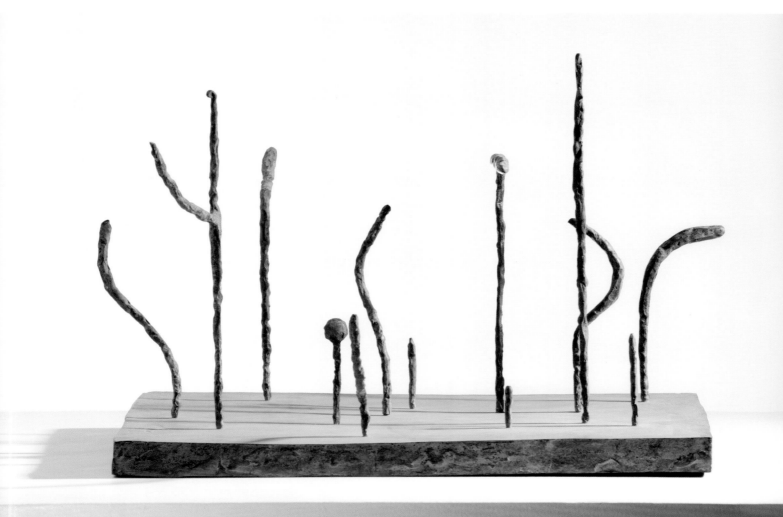

5

Playground (Game)
1949
bronze
cast no.2 from an edition of 4 plus 1 artist's cast
4 ½ × 19 × 27 ½ in / 11·4 × 48·3 × 70 cm

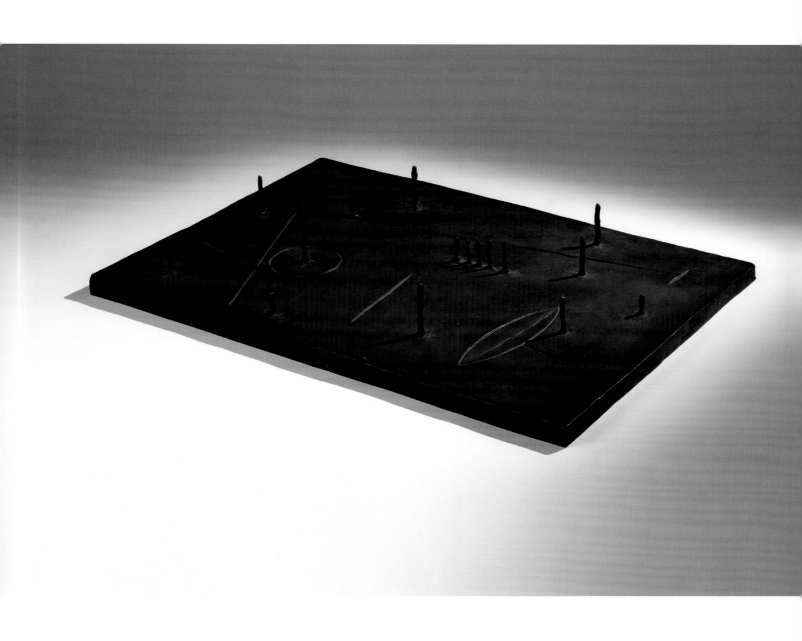

6

Head
1950
bronze
artist's cast no.1 of 1, edition of 4
26¾ × 14 × 15⅜ in / 67·9 × 35·6 × 39 cm

7

Acrobat
1951
bronze
cast no.3 from an edition of 4
43¾ × 32 × 22 in / 111·1 × 81·3 × 55·9 cm
on stone base

8

Horse
1950
bronze
cast no.6 from an edition of 6 plus 1 artist's cast
30 ¾ × 37 ½ × 24 ½ in / 78·1 × 95·3 × 62·2 cm

9

Pegasus
1954
bronze
artist's cast no.1 of 1, edition of 4
35 × 17 ½ × 29 in / 88·9 × 44·5 × 73·7 cm

10

Relief 2
1955
bronze
one cast from an unnumbered edition of 2
1 × 15 ¼ × 23 ¼ in / 2·5 × 38·7 × 59 cm

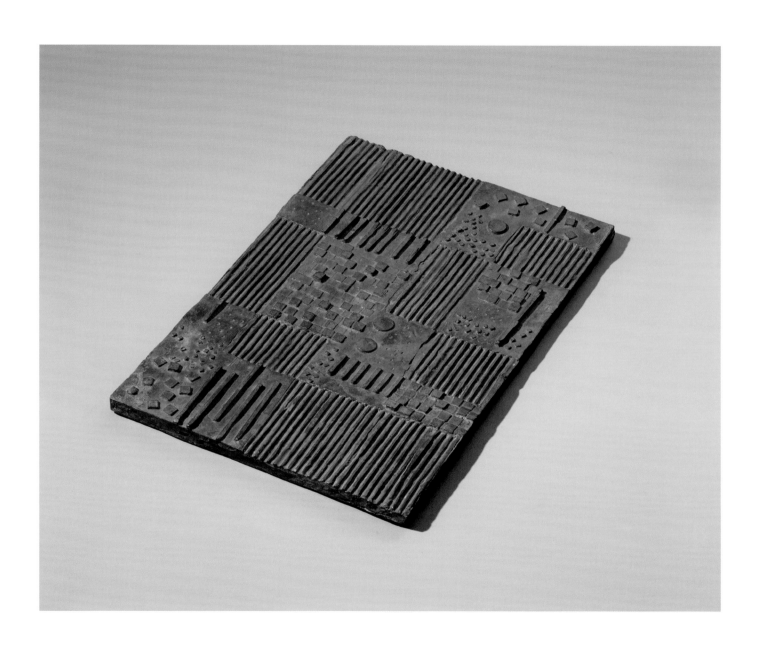

11

Relief 5
1955
bronze
one cast from an unnumbered edition of 2
2 ¼ × 15 ½ × 23 ½ in / 5·7 × 39·4 × 59·7 cm

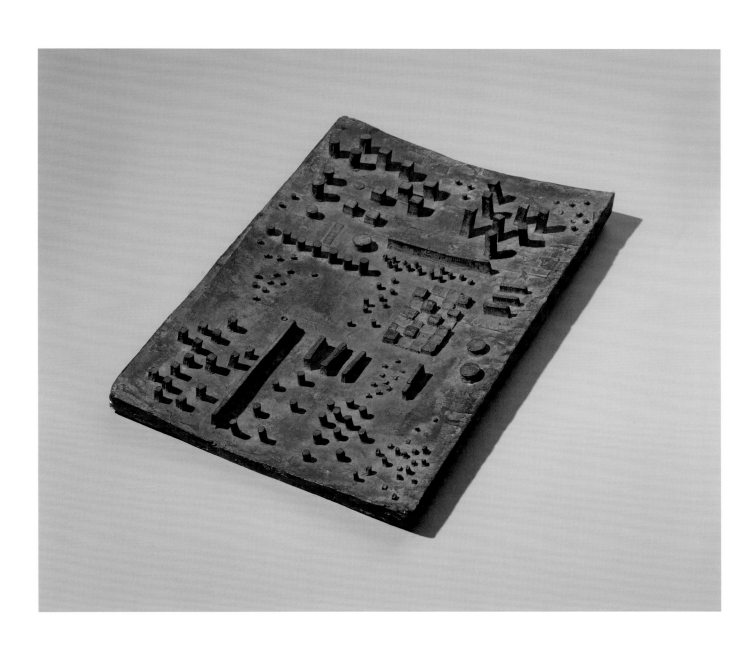

12

Figure
1955
bronze
cast no.1 from an edition of 4 plus 1 artist's cast
42 ¼ × 7 ½ × 15 ⅜ in / 107·3 × 19 × 39 cm

13

Eve 1
1959
bronze and rosewood, unique
61 ½ × 15 in diameter / 156·2 × 38·1 cm diameter

14

Lotus Totem
1962
bronze and rosewood, unique
77 × 15 in diameter / 195·6 × 38·1 cm diameter

15

Sculpture
1956
bronze
cast no.4 from an edition of 4 plus 1 artist's cast
58 × 49 × 15 in / 147·3 × 124·5 × 38·1 cm

16

Tall Balance
1992
bronze
cast no.5 from an edition of 6 plus 1 artist's cast
61 ¼ × 71 × 11 in / 155·6 × 180 × 28 cm

17

Small Spade Venus
1986
bronze
cast no.6 from an edition of 6 plus 1 artist's cast
35⅜ × 17 × 1½ in / 89·8 × 43 × 4 cm
on York stone base

18

Large Blade Venus
1990
bronze
cast no.5 from an edition of 5 plus 1 artist's cast
125 × 39 × 26 ¾ in / 317·5 × 99·1 × 68 cm

19

Female
1989
bronze
artist's cast no.1 of 1, edition of 6
75 ½ × 20 ½ × 12 ½ in / 191·8 × 52 × 31·7 cm

20

Female
1990
bronze
cast no.6 from an edition of 6 plus 1 artist's cast
66½ × 16½ × 12½ in / 168·9 × 41·9 × 31·7 cm

21

Female Figure
1991
bronze
cast no.2 from an edition of 6 plus 1 artist's cast
81 ½ × 12 ¾ × 16 ½ in / 207 × 32·4 × 41·9 cm

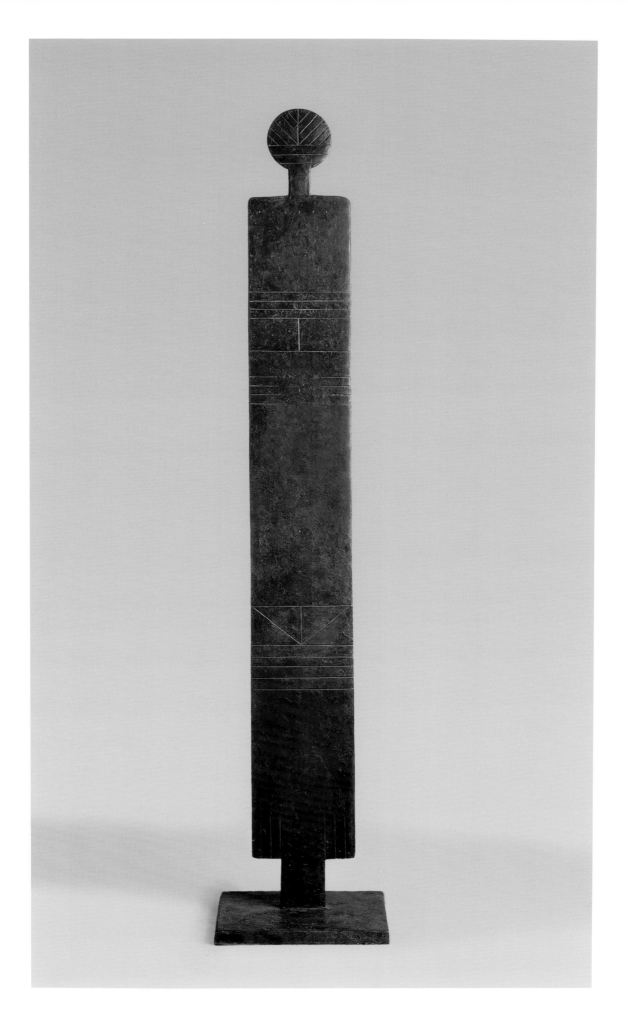

22

Paddle Venus 3
1986
bronze
cast no.5 from an edition of 6 plus 1 artist's cast
73 ¼ × 14 ¼ × 19 ½ in / 186 × 36·2 × 49·5 cm
on bronze base

23

Large Metamorphic Venus
1982
bronze
cast no.3 from an edition of 6 plus 1 artist's cast
68 ¾ × 31 × 10 in / 174·6 × 78·7 × 25·4 cm
on bronze base

24

Horse 5
1988
bronze
cast no.1 from an edition of 6 plus 1 artist's cast
28 ¾ × 37 ¼ × 13 ⅛ in / 73 × 94·6 × 33·3 cm
on York stone base

25

Horse
1999
bronze
cast no.1 from an edition of 6 plus 1 artist's cast
71 ½ × 29 × 80 ¾ in / 181·5 × 73·6 × 205·1 cm

26

Large Horse
1990
bronze
cast no.2 from an edition of 5 plus 1 artist's cast
115 × 139 × 54 ½ in / 292 × 353 × 138·4 cm

27

Untitled
1957
oil on canvas
60 × 45 in / 152·4 × 114·3 cm

28

Untitled
1957
oil on canvas
60 × 45 in / 152·4 × 114·3 cm

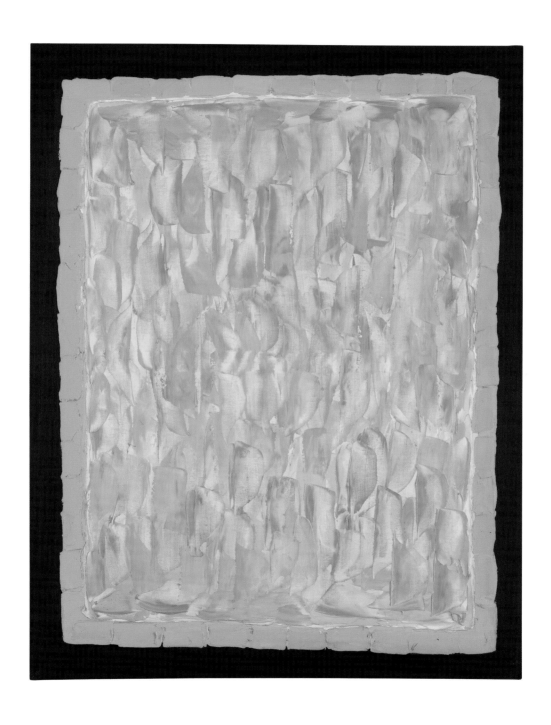

29

Untitled
1957
oil on canvas
60 × 45 in / 152·4 × 114·3 cm

30

24–1958
oil on canvas
78 × 58 in / 198·1 × 147·3 cm

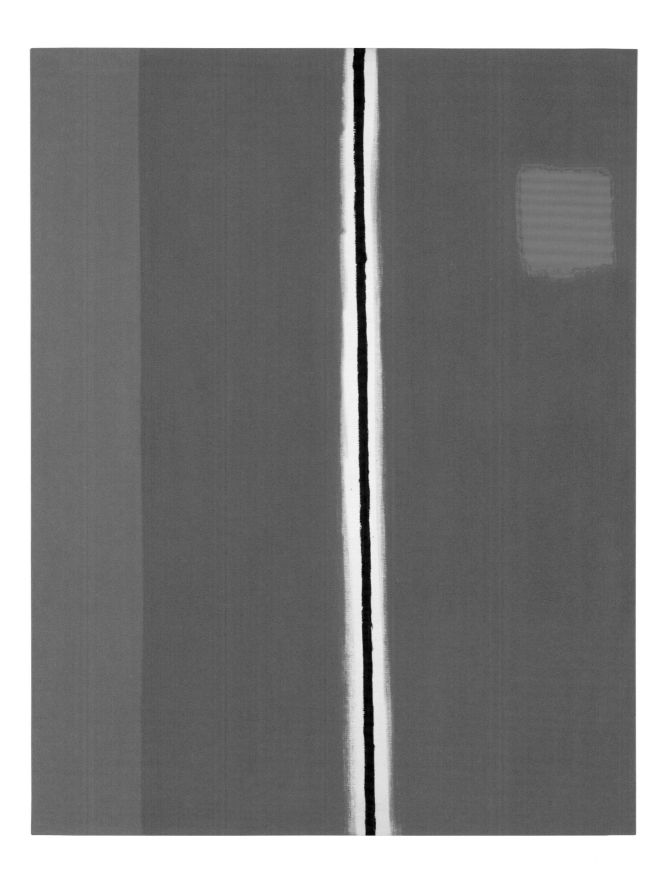

31

23–1958
oil on canvas
78 × 58 in / 198·1 × 147·3 cm

32

9–1959
oil on canvas
70 × 70 in / 177·8 × 177·8 cm

33

5–1959
oil on canvas
60 × 60 in / 152·4 × 152·4 cm

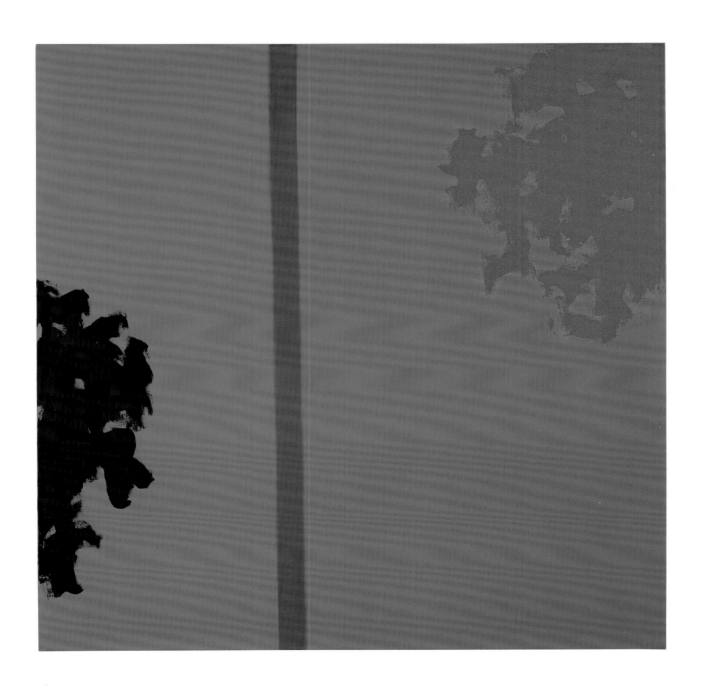

34

12–1960
oil on canvas
72 × 60 in / 183 × 152·4 cm

LIST OF WORKS

1
Mask
1946
bronze
cast no.4 from an edition of 4
plus 1 artist's cast
15 ½ × 9 ¼ × ⅝ in / 39·4 × 23·5 × 1·6 cm
on York stone base

stamped with the artist's monogram,
inscribed with cast and edition number
"4/4" and date "46" on reverse

Provenance
The artist

Exhibited
'William Turnbull: Retrospective 1946–2003',
  Yorkshire Sculpture Park, West Bretton,
  Wakefield, 14 May–9 October 2005
  (exhibition guide p.5, repro. in colour p.[4],
  fig.3) (artist's cast exhibited)
'William Turnbull: Sculpture and Paintings
  1946–1962', Waddington Galleries, London,
  31 January–24 February 2007, catalogue
  no.1 (repro. in colour p.5) (artist's cast
  exhibited)

Literature
William Turnbull: sculpture and painting,
  Richard Morphet, Tate Gallery
  Publications, London, 1973, p.31 (repro. in
  b&w p.22, fig.2)
'William Turnbull: A Consistent Way of
  Thinking', Patrick Elliott, in *William
  Turnbull: sculpture and paintings*, David
  Sylvester (intro.), Merrell Holberton
  Publishers, in association with
  Serpentine Gallery, London, 1995, p.14
  (not repro.)
The Sculpture of William Turnbull, Amanda
  A. Davidson, The Henry Moore Foundation
  in association with Lund Humphries, 2005,
  catalogue no.3, pp.12 & 79 (repro. in b&w
  p.79)

2
Heavy Insect
1949
bronze
cast no.4 from an edition of 4
plus 1 artist's cast
20 ½ × 33 ¼ × 8 ¾ in / 52 × 84·5 × 22·2 cm

stamped with the artist's monogram,
inscribed with cast and edition number
"4/4" and date "49" on underside, at tail end

Provenance
The artist

Exhibited
'William Turnbull: sculpture and painting',
  The Tate Gallery, London, 15 August–7
  October 1973, catalogue no.4, pp.23–24
  (repro. in b&w p.23) (artist's cast
  exhibited)
'William Turnbull: Retrospective 1946–2003',
  Yorkshire Sculpture Park, West Bretton,
  Wakefield, 14 May–9 October 2005
  (exhibition guide p.6, repro. in colour p.[7],
  fig.10) (artist's cast exhibited)
'William Turnbull', Duveen Galleries, Tate
  Britain, London, 14 June–26 November
  2006 (artist's cast exhibited)

Literature
'William Turnbull: A Consistent Way of
  Thinking', Patrick Elliott, in *William
  Turnbull: sculpture and paintings*, David
  Sylvester (intro.), Merrell Holberton
  Publishers, in association with
  Serpentine Gallery, London, 1995, p.18
  (repro. in b&w p.15, pl.4)
The Sculpture of William Turnbull, Amanda
  A. Davidson, The Henry Moore Foundation
  in association with Lund Humphries,
  2005, catalogue no.14, pp.19–20 & 81
  (repro. in b&w p.19, fig.7)

3
Hanging Sculpture
1949
plaster over wire
(to be cast in a bronze edition of 6 plus
1 artist's cast)
48 in / 121·9 cm wide

Provenance
The artist

Literature
William Turnbull: sculpture and painting,
Richard Morphet, Tate Gallery
Publications, London, 1973, pp.23–24
(repro. in b&w p.23, fig.3)
'William Turnbull: A Consistent Way of
Thinking', Patrick Elliott, in *William
Turnbull: sculpture and paintings*, David
Sylvester (intro.), Merrell Holberton
Publishers, in association with
Serpentine Gallery, London, 1995, p.18
(not repro.)
The Sculpture of William Turnbull, Amanda
A. Davidson, The Henry Moore Foundation
in association with Lund Humphries, 2005,
catalogue no.8, pp.21 & 80 (repro. in b&w
p.[15], fig.4)

4
Forms on a Base
1949
bronze, unique
13 ¼ × 13 ½ × 18 ½ in / 33·7 × 34·3 × 47 cm

Provenance
The artist

Exhibited
'William Turnbull: sculpture and painting',
The Tate Gallery, London, 15 August–7
October 1973, catalogue no.5, pp.23–24
& 27 (repro. in b&w p.26)
'William Turnbull: Retrospective 1946–2003',
Yorkshire Sculpture Park, West Bretton,
Wakefield, 14 May–9 October 2005
(exhibition guide p.6, repro. in colour
p.[7], fig.9)

Literature
'William Turnbull: A Consistent Way of
Thinking', Patrick Elliott, in *William
Turnbull: sculpture and paintings*, David
Sylvester (intro.), Merrell Holberton
Publishers, in association with Serpentine
Gallery, London, 1995, p.18 (not repro.)
'William Turnbull: Painter and Sculptor',
Bernard Cohen, *Modern Painters*,
Winter 1995, pp.30–35 (repro.; titled
'Sculpture') (previously publ. in *Studio
International*, vol.186, July–August 1973,
pp.9–16)
The Sculpture of William Turnbull, Amanda
A. Davidson, The Henry Moore Foundation
in association with Lund Humphries,
2005, catalogue no.15, p.82 (repro. in
b&w p.82) (noted as 'maquette for large
sculpture')

5
Playground (Game)
1949
bronze
cast no.2 from an edition of 4
plus 1 artist's cast
4 ½ × 19 × 27 ½ in / 11·4 × 48·3 × 70 cm

stamped with the artist's monogram,
inscribed with cast and edition number
"2/4" and date "49" on edge

Provenance
The artist

Exhibited
'William Turnbull: sculpture and painting',
The Tate Gallery, London, 15 August–7
October 1973, catalogue no.6, pp.23–24,
27, 29, 34, 44 & 56 (repro. in b&w p.27)
'Play/Ground: William Turnbull and the
Horizontal Relief', Henry Moore Institute,
Leeds, 6 November 2004–6 February 2005
(repro. in b&w in exhibition leaflet)
'William Turnbull: Retrospective 1946–2003',
Yorkshire Sculpture Park, West Bretton,
Wakefield, 14 May–9 October 2005,
exhibition guide pp.6 & 10 (repro. in colour
p.6, fig.8) (artist's cast exhibited)

Literature

'Sculpture as Walls and Playgrounds',
Lawrence Alloway, *Architectural Design*
27, January 1957, p.26 (repro. in b&w)

'William Turnbull: In Space', in *Transition:
The London Art Scene in the Fifties*, Martin
Harrison, Merrell Publishers in
association with Barbican Art Galleries,
London, 2002, pp.111–112 (not repro.)

William Turnbull, Waddington Galleries,
London, 2004 (repro. in colour pp.[6–7])

The Sculpture of William Turnbull, Amanda
A. Davidson, The Henry Moore Foundation
in association with Lund Humphries,
2005, catalogue no.16, pp.16–17, 20 & 82
(repro. in b&w p.82)

One cast of this sculpture is in the collection
of Leeds Museums and Galleries, Leeds

6
Head

1950
bronze
artist's cast no.1 of 1, edition of 4
26¾ × 14 × 15⅜ in / 67·9 × 35·6 × 39 cm

Provenance
The artist

Exhibited

'New Aspects of British Sculpture', British
Council exhibition, The British Pavilion,
The XXVI Biennale, Venice, 14 June–19
October 1952, catalogue no.149 (dated
1951) (not repro.) (artist's cast exhibited)

'William Turnbull: Retrospective 1946–2003',
Yorkshire Sculpture Park, West Bretton,
Wakefield, 14 May–9 October 2005 (artist's
cast exhibited)

Literature

British Sculpture in the Twentieth Century,
Sandy Nairne and Nicholas Serota (eds.),
Whitechapel Art Gallery, London, 1981
(repro. in b&w installation photograph
of British Pavilion at 1952 Venice Biennale,
p.144)

'William Turnbull: In Space', in *Transition:
The London Art Scene in the Fifties*, Martin
Harrison, Merrell Publishers in association
with Barbican Art Galleries, London, 2002
(repro. in b&w on frontispiece)

The Sculpture of William Turnbull, Amanda
A. Davidson, The Henry Moore Foundation
in association with Lund Humphries,
2005, catalogue no.19, pp.21–22 & 83
(repro. in b&w p.21, fig.9)

7
Acrobat

1951
bronze
cast no.3 from an edition of 4
43¾ × 32 × 22 in / 111·1 × 81·3 × 55·9 cm
on stone base

stamped with the artist's monogram,
inscribed with cast and edition number
"3/4" and date "51" on side of foot

Provenance
The artist

Exhibited

'William Turnbull: Sculptures 1946–62, 1985–
87', Waddington Galleries, London, 28
October–21 November 1987, catalogue
no.2 (repro. in colour p.15)

'Post War Sculpture', Arnold Herstand &
Company, New York, 14 July–September
1989 (2/4 exhibited)

'William Turnbull: Recent Sculpture', Arnold
Herstand & Company, New York, 19
October–22 November 1989 (repro.
in colour on announcement card)
(2/4 exhibited)

'William Turnbull', Galerie Michael Haas,
Berlin, 17 October–28 November 1992
(not repro. in catalogue) (4/4 exhibited)

'Transition: The London Art Scene in the
Fifties', Barbican Gallery, Barbican
Centre, London, 31 January–14 April 2002,
catalogue no.101, p.111 (repro. in b&w
p.113) (3/4 exhibited)

'William Turnbull: Retrospective 1946–2003',
Yorkshire Sculpture Park, West Bretton,
Wakefield, 14 May–9 October 2005
(exhibition guide p.6, not repro.)
(3/4 exhibited)
'William Turnbull', Duveen Galleries, Tate
Britain, London, 14 June–26 November
2006 (3/4 exhibited)

Literature
*The Battle for Realism: Figurative Art in
Britain During the Cold War 1945–1960*,
James Hyman, Yale University Press,
New Haven and London, 2001 (repro. in
b&w p.30, fig.23)
The Sculpture of William Turnbull, Amanda
A. Davidson, The Henry Moore
Foundation in association with Lund
Humphries, 2005, catalogue no.22, pp.20 &
83 (repro. in b&w p.83)

8
Horse
1950
bronze
cast no.6 from an edition of 6
plus 1 artist's cast
30 ¾ × 37 ½ × 24 ½ in / 78·1 × 95·3 × 62·2 cm

stamped with the artist's monogram and
inscribed with cast and edition number
"6/6" on back right leg

Provenance
The artist

Exhibited
'New Aspects of British Sculpture', British
Council exhibition, The British Pavilion,
The XXVI Biennale, Venice, 14 June–19
October 1952, catalogue no.150 (dated
1951) (not repro.) (artist's cast exhibited)
'The Independent Group: Postwar Britain
and the Aesthetics of Plenty', Institute of
Contemporary Arts, London, 1 February–
1 April 1990; touring to IVAM Centro Julio
González, Valencia, 16 May–16 September
1990; The Museum of Contemporary Art,

Los Angeles, 4 November 1990–13
January 1991; University Art Museum,
University of California at Berkeley, 6
February–21 April 1991; Hood Museum
of Art, Dartmouth College, Hanover,
New Hampshire, 8 June–18 August 1991,
catalogue no.74, p.118 (repro. in b&w)
(artist's cast exhibited)
'William Turnbull: Horses–Development of a
Theme, Other Sculptures and Paintings',
Waddington Galleries, London, 22 June–
20 July 2001, catalogue no.2 (repro. in
colour p.[7]) (3/6 exhibited)
'Henry Moore and the Geometry of Fear',
James Hyman Fine Art, London,
19 November 2002–18 January 2003,
catalogue no.29, p.47 (repro. in
colour; installation photograph fig.1)
(3/6 exhibited)
'William Turnbull: Retrospective 1946–2003',
Yorkshire Sculpture Park, West Bretton,
Wakefield, 14 May–9 October 2005
(1/6 exhibited)
'William Turnbull', Duveen Galleries, Tate
Britain, London, 14 June–26 November
2006 (artist's cast exhibited)
'William Turnbull: Sculpture and Paintings
1946–1962', Waddington Galleries,
London, 31 January–24 February 2007,
catalogue no.2 (repro. in colour p.7) (5/6
exhibited)

Literature
William Turnbull: sculpture and painting,
Richard Morphet, Tate Gallery
Publications, London, 1973 (repro. in
b&w p.27, fig.7)
British Sculpture in the Twentieth Century,
Sandy Nairne and Nicholas Serota (eds.),
Whitechapel Art Gallery, London, 1981
(repro. in b&w installation photograph of
British Pavilion at 1952 Venice Biennale,
p.144)
'William Turnbull: A Consistent Way of
Thinking', Patrick Elliott, in *William
Turnbull: sculpture and paintings*, David
Sylvester (intro.), Merrell Holberton
Publishers, in association with
Serpentine Gallery, London, 1995, p.18
(not repro.)

William Turnbull, Waddington Galleries, London, 2004 (repro. in colour p.[9]) (incorrectly dated)

The Sculpture of William Turnbull, Amanda A. Davidson, The Henry Moore Foundation in association with Lund Humphries, 2005, catalogue no.20, pp.20–23 & 83 (repro. in b&w p.20, fig.8)

One cast of this sculpture is in the Tate Collection, London

9
Pegasus
1954
bronze
artist's cast no.1 of 1, edition of 4
35 × 17 ½ × 29 in / 88·9 × 44·5 × 73·7 cm

inscribed "Turnbull 54" at base

Provenance
The artist

Exhibited
'William Turnbull: sculpture and painting', The Tate Gallery, London, 15 August–7 October 1973, catalogue no.15, pp.28–29, 34 & 39 (repro. in b&w p.28) (artist's cast exhibited)

'William Turnbull: Sculptures 1946–62, 1985–87', Waddington Galleries, London, 28 October–21 November 1987, catalogue no.3 (repro. in colour p.17) (artist's cast exhibited)

'Scottish Art since 1900', Scottish National Gallery of Modern Art, Edinburgh, 17 June–24 September 1989; touring to Barbican Art Gallery, London, 8 February–16 April 1990, catalogue no.334, p.167 (repro. in colour p.79) (1/4 exhibited)

'William Turnbull: Horses–Development of a Theme, Other Sculptures and Paintings', Waddington Galleries, London, 22 June–20 July 2001, catalogue no.3 (repro. in colour p.[9]) (1/4 exhibited)

'William Turnbull: Paintings 1959–1963, Bronze Sculpture 1954–1958', Waddington Galleries, London, 24 November–22 December 2004, catalogue no.14 (repro. in colour) (2/4 exhibited)

'William Turnbull: Retrospective 1946–2003', Yorkshire Sculpture Park, West Bretton, Wakefield, 14 May–9 October 2005 (exhibition guide p.5, not repro.) (artist's cast exhibited)

Literature
'William Turnbull', Richard Morphet, in *The Alistair McAlpine Gift*, Tate Gallery Publications, London, 1971, p.106 (not repro.)

'William Turnbull: A Consistent Way of Thinking', Patrick Elliott, in *William Turnbull: sculpture and paintings*, David Sylvester (intro.), Merrell Holberton Publishers, in association with Serpentine Gallery, London, 1995, p.26 (repro. in b&w p.17, pl.6)

William Turnbull, Waddington Galleries, London, 2004 (repro. in colour p.[11])

The Sculpture of William Turnbull, Amanda A. Davidson, The Henry Moore Foundation in association with Lund Humphries, 2005, catalogue no.37, pp.29 & 88 (repro. in b&w p.29, fig.13)

10
Relief 2
1955
bronze
one cast from an unnumbered edition of 2
1 × 15 ¼ × 23 ¼ in / 2·5 × 38·7 × 59 cm

Provenance
The artist

Exhibited
'William Turnbull: New Sculpture and Paintings', ICA Gallery, London, 25 September–2 November 1957, catalogue no.18 (not repro.)

'William Turnbull: sculpture and painting',
  The Tate Gallery, London, 15 August–7
  October 1973, catalogue no.17 (repro. in
  b&w p.29 and with 'Relief 1', fig.8)

Literature
'Sculpture as Walls and Playgrounds',
  Lawrence Alloway, *Architectural Design*
  27, January 1957, p.26 (repro. in b&w)
The Sculpture of William Turnbull, Amanda
  A. Davidson, The Henry Moore Foundation
  in association with Lund Humphries,
  2005, catalogue no.44, pp.32 & 90 (repro. in
  b&w p.90)

11
Relief 5
1955
bronze
one cast from an unnumbered edition of 2
2 ¼ × 15 ½ × 23 ½ in / 5·7 × 39·4 × 59·7 cm

Provenance
The artist

Exhibited
'William Turnbull: sculpture and painting',
  The Tate Gallery, London, 15 August–7
  October 1973, catalogue no.19 (repro. in
  b&w p.29)
'William Turnbull: Retrospective 1946–2003',
  Yorkshire Sculpture Park, West Bretton,
  Wakefield, 14 May–9 October 2005
  (exhibition guide p.6, not repro.)
'Close Encounters: The Sculptor's Studio in
  the Age of the Camera', Henry Moore
  Institute, Leeds, 27 September 2001–6
  January 2002, catalogue no.73, p.27 (repro.
  in b&w)

Literature
'Sculpture as Walls and Playgrounds',
  Lawrence Alloway, *Architectural Design*
  27, January 1957, p.26 (repro. in b&w)
The Sculpture of William Turnbull, Amanda
  A. Davidson, The Henry Moore Foundation
  in association with Lund Humphries,
  2005, catalogue no.47, pp.32 & 90 (repro. in
  b&w p.91)

12
Figure
1955
bronze
cast no.1 from an edition of 4
plus 1 artist's cast
42 ¼ × 7 ½ × 15 ⅜ in / 107·3 × 19 × 39 cm

stamped with the artist's monogram,
inscribed with cast and edition number
"1/4" and date "55" on surface of base,
back right

Provenance
The artist

Exhibited
'William Turnbull: New Sculpture and
  Paintings', ICA Gallery, London, 25
  September–2 November 1957, catalogue
  no.14 (plaster repro. in b&w) (titled
  'Standing Male Figure')
'William Turnbull: Retrospective 1946–2003',
  Yorkshire Sculpture Park, West Bretton,
  Wakefield, 14 May–9 October 2005 (artist's
  cast exhibited)
'William Turnbull: Sculpture and Paintings
  1946–1962', Waddington Galleries, London,
  31 January–24 February 2007, catalogue
  no.3 (repro. in colour p.9) (artist's cast
  exhibited)

Literature
The Sculpture of William Turnbull, Amanda
  A. Davidson, The Henry Moore Foundation
  in association with Lund Humphries,
  2005, catalogue no.59, p.95 (repro. in b&w
  p.95)

13
Eve 1
1959
bronze and rosewood, unique
61 ½ × 15 in diameter /
156·2 × 38·1 cm diameter

stamped with the artist's monogram and
dated "59" at base of bronze part

Provenance
E J Power
Thence by family descent

Exhibited
'William Turnbull: Sculpture', Molton
    Gallery, London, 19 April–6 May 1960,
    catalogue no.9 (repro. in b&w) (incorrectly
    captioned 'Eve 2')
'William Turnbull: sculpture and painting',
    The Tate Gallery, London, 15 August–7
    October 1973, catalogue no.47, p.40 (repro.
    in b&w p.41)

Literature
'Expositions: Grande-Bretagne', review
    of Molton Gallery exhibition, J.P. Hodin,
    *Quadrum: Revue Internationale d'Art
    Moderne*, no.11, December 1961, p.175
    (repro. in b&w)
'The Sculpture and Painting of William
    Turnbull', Lawrence Alloway, *Art
    International*, vol.5, no.1, 1 February 1961,
    pp.46–52 (repro. in b&w p.47, fig.4)
The Sculpture of William Turnbull, Amanda
    A. Davidson, The Henry Moore Foundation
    in association with Lund Humphries,
    2005, catalogue no.93, pp.50 & 108 (repro.
    in b&w p.108)

14
Lotus Totem
1962
bronze and rosewood, unique
77 × 15 in diameter /
195·6 × 38·1 cm diameter

stamped with the artist's monogram and
inscribed with date "62" on underside of
head and on side of base

Provenance
Alistair McAlpine
Anon. sale, Sotheby's, London: 7 November
    1990 (lot no.186)
New Art Centre, Roche Court, Nr. Salisbury,
    Wiltshire
Private Collection, USA

Exhibited
'Turnbull', Marlborough-Gerson Gallery,
    New York, October 1963, catalogue no.4
    (repro. in b&w)
'William Turnbull: sculpture and painting',
    The Tate Gallery, London, 15 August–7
    October 1973, catalogue no.53, p.43 (repro.
    in b&w p.42)

Literature
The Sculpture of William Turnbull, Amanda
    A. Davidson, The Henry Moore Foundation
    in association with Lund Humphries,
    2005, catalogue no.115, p.117 (repro. in
    b&w p.117)

15
Sculpture
1956
bronze
cast no.4 from an edition of 4
plus 1 artist's cast
58 × 49 × 15 in / 147·3 × 124·5 × 38·1 cm

inscribed with the artist's monogram, cast
and edition number "4/4" and date "56" at
base

Provenance
The artist

Exhibited
'William Turnbull: Sculpture and Painting',
    Pavilion Gallery, Balboa, California, 13
    March–24 April 1966, catalogue no.5
    (not repro.)

'William Turnbull: sculpture and painting',
The Tate Gallery, London, 15 August–7
October 1973, catalogue no.32, pp.37 &
41 (repro. in b&w p.37)

'William Turnbull: Sculptures 1946–62, 1985–
87', Waddington Galleries, London, 28
October–21 November 1987, catalogue
no.8 (repro. in colour p.27)

'William Turnbull: Paintings 1959–1963,
Bronze Sculpture 1954–1958', Waddington
Galleries, London, 24 November–22
December 2004, catalogue no.15 (repro.
in colour) (artist's cast exhibited)

'William Turnbull: Retrospective 1946–2003',
Yorkshire Sculpture Park, West Bretton,
Wakefield, 14 May–9 October 2005 (artist's
cast exhibited)

'William Turnbull: Sculpture and Paintings
1946–1962', Waddington Galleries, London,
31 January–24 February 2007, catalogue
no.5 (repro. in colour p.13) (2/4 exhibited)

Literature

The Sculpture of William Turnbull, Amanda
A. Davidson, The Henry Moore Foundation
in association with Lund Humphries, 2005,
catalogue no.71, p.99 (repro. in b&w p.99)

16
Tall Balance
1992
bronze
cast no.5 from an edition of 6
plus 1 artist's cast
61 ¼ × 71 × 11 in / 155·6 × 180 × 28 cm

stamped with the artist's monogram,
inscribed with cast and edition number
"5/6" and date "92" on base

Provenance
The artist

Exhibited
'Works on Paper and Sculpture', Waddington
Galleries, London, 8 September–2 October
1993 (ex-catalogue) (2/6 exhibited)

'William Turnbull: Bronze Idols and Untitled
Paintings', Serpentine Gallery, London,

15 November 1995–7 January 1996 (4/6
exhibited)

'British Figurative Art–Part Two: Sculpture',
Flowers East, London, 6 August–20
September 1998 (repro. in b&w p.[89])
(4/6 exhibited)

'William Turnbull: Retrospective 1946–2003',
Yorkshire Sculpture Park, West Bretton,
Wakefield, 14 May–9 October 2005 (artist's
cast exhibited)

Literature

William Turnbull: sculpture and paintings,
David Sylvester (intro.) and Patrick Elliott,
Merrell Holberton Publishers, in
association with Serpentine Gallery,
London, 1995 (repro. in b&w p.86, pl.64)

'William Turnbull: Painter and Sculptor',
Bernard Cohen, *Modern Painters*, Winter
1995, pp.30–35 (repro. in colour p.35)
(previously publ. in *Studio International*,
vol.186, July–August 1973, pp.9–16)

*British Art: A selection from Waddington
Galleries*, Waddington Galleries, London,
1997, no.40 (repro. in colour)

'William Turnbull in conversation with Colin
Renfrew', in *William Turnbull: Sculpture
and Paintings*, Waddington Galleries,
London, 1998, p.8 (repro. in b&w p.9)

Contemporary Sculpture in Scotland,
Andrew Patrizio, Craftsman House,
Sydney, 1999, p.131 (repro. in b&w)

William Turnbull, Waddington Galleries,
London, 2004 (repro. in colour p.[37])

The Sculpture of William Turnbull, Amanda
A. Davidson, The Henry Moore Foundation
in association with Lund Humphries,
2005, catalogue no.285, pp.71 & 184 (repro.
in b&w p.70, fig.38)

17
Small Spade Venus
1986
bronze
cast no.6 from an edition of 6
plus 1 artist's cast
35 ⅜ × 17 × 1 ½ in / 89·8 × 43 × 4 cm
on York stone base

stamped with the artist's monogram,
inscribed with cast and edition number
"6/6" and date "86" at base

Provenance
The artist

Exhibited
'William Turnbull: Sculptures 1946–62, 1985–
  87', Waddington Galleries, London, 28
  October–21 November 1987, catalogue
  no.23 (repro. in colour p.59)
'William Turnbull Sculptures', Terry
  Dintenfass Inc., New York, 5 March–
  2 April 1988
'Recent Sculpture: William Turnbull', John
  Berggruen Gallery, San Francisco,
  3 November 1988–7 January 1989
'William Turnbull', Galerie Michael Haas,
  Berlin, 17 October–28 November 1992,
  catalogue no.7 (repro. in colour) (3/6
  exhibited)
'William Turnbull: Skulpturen (1979–1991)',
  Galerie Sander, Darmstadt, 8 April–
  21 May 1994
'William Turnbull', Barbara Mathes Gallery,
  New York, 15 October–28 November 1998
  (3/6 exhibited)
'William Turnbull: Sculpture', Barbara
  Mathes Gallery, New York, 26 April–
  28 June 2002 (3/6 exhibited)

Literature
The Sculpture of William Turnbull, Amanda
  A. Davidson, The Henry Moore Foundation
  in association with Lund Humphries,
  2005, catalogue no.243, p.169 (repro. in
  b&w p.169)

18
Large Blade Venus
1990
bronze
cast no.5 from an edition of 5
plus 1 artist's cast
125 × 39 × 26 ¾ in / 317·5 × 99·1 × 68 cm

stamped with the artist's monogram,
inscribed with cast and edition number
"5/5" and date "90" at base

Provenance
The artist

Exhibited
'William Turnbull: Recent Sculpture',
  Waddington Galleries, London, 25
  September–19 October 1991, catalogue
  no.17 (repro. in colour p.39) (1/5 exhibited)
'William Turnbull: Bronze Idols and Untitled
  Paintings', Serpentine Gallery, London,
  15 November 1995–7 January 1996
  (3/5 exhibited)
'Sculpture in the Close', Quincentenary
  Exhibition, Jesus College, Cambridge, 22
  September–29 October 1996 (repro. in
  colour in catalogue) (3/5 exhibited)
'Pour l'amour de Vénus', Donjon de Vez, Vez,
  France, 14 June–5 October 2003,
  catalogue p.18 (repro. in colour p.19) (3/5
  exhibited)
'William Turnbull: Retrospective 1946–2003',
  Yorkshire Sculpture Park, West Bretton,
  Wakefield, 14 May–9 October 2005 (repro.
  in colour in exhibition guide p.[24], fig.43)
  (3/5 exhibited)

Literature
William Turnbull: sculpture and paintings,
  David Sylvester (intro.) and Patrick Elliott,
  Merrell Holberton Publishers, in
  association with Serpentine Gallery,
  London, 1995 (repro. in colour p.90, pl.68)
The Sculpture of William Turnbull, Amanda
  A. Davidson, The Henry Moore Foundation
  in association with Lund Humphries,
  2005, catalogue no.274, pp.23 & 179 (repro.
  in b&w p.179)

One cast of this sculpture is in the collection of The Fitzwilliam Museum, Cambridge, gifted by the National Art Collections Fund in 2006

19
Female
1989
bronze
artist's cast no.1 of 1, edition of 6
75 ½ × 20 ½ × 12 ½ in / 191·8 × 52 × 31·7 cm

stamped with the artist's monogram, inscribed with cast "A/C" and date "89" on back of base

Provenance
The artist

Exhibited
'William Turnbull: Recent Sculpture', Waddington Galleries, London, 25 September–19 October 1991, catalogue no.10 (repro. in colour p.25) (5/6 exhibited)
'William Turnbull', Galeria Freites, Caracas, 18 October–10 November 1992 (repro. in colour in catalogue p.25) (6/6 exhibited)
'William Turnbull', Galerie Michael Haas Berlin, 17 October–28 November 1992 (not repro. in catalogue) (5/6 exhibited)
'William Turnbull: Skulpturen', Galerie Thomas, Munich, 5 April–19 June 2002 (repro. in colour in catalogue p.6) (2/6 exhibited)
'William Turnbull: Retrospective 1946–2003', Yorkshire Sculpture Park, West Bretton, Wakefield, 14 May–9 October 2005 (exhibition guide p.18, not repro.) (artist's cast exhibited)

Literature
The Sculpture of William Turnbull, Amanda A. Davidson, The Henry Moore Foundation in association with Lund Humphries, 2005, catalogue no.265, p.176 (repro. in b&w p.176)

20
Female
1990
bronze
cast no.6 from an edition of 6
plus 1 artist's cast
66 ½ × 16 ½ × 12 ½ in / 168·9 × 41·9 × 31·7 cm

stamped with the artist's monogram, inscribed with cast and edition number "6/6" and date "90" at base

Provenance
The artist

Exhibited
'William Turnbull: Recent Sculpture', Waddington Galleries, London, 25 September–19 October 1991, catalogue no.15 (repro. in colour p.35) (1/6 exhibited)
'William Turnbull', Galeria Freites, Caracas, 18 October–10 November 1992 (repro. in colour in catalogue p.27) (1/6 exhibited)
'William Turnbull', Galerie Michael Haas, Berlin, 17 October–28 November 1992, catalogue no.14 (repro. in colour) (2/6 exhibited)
'William Turnbull: Skulpturen (1979–1991)', Galerie Sander, Darmstadt, 8 April–21 May 1994 (2/6 exhibited)
'William Turnbull: Bronze Idols and Untitled Paintings', Serpentine Gallery, London, 15 November 1995–7 January 1996 (1/6 exhibited)

Literature
William Turnbull: sculpture and paintings, David Sylvester (intro.) and Patrick Elliott, Merrell Holberton Publishers, in association with Serpentine Gallery, London, 1995 (repro. in colour p.87, pl.65)
Contemporary Sculpture in Scotland, Andrew Patrizio, Craftsman House, Sydney, 1999, p.128 (repro. in colour)
The Sculpture of William Turnbull, Amanda A. Davidson, The Henry Moore Foundation in association with Lund Humphries, 2005, catalogue no.275, p.179 (repro. in b&w p.179)

21
Female Figure
1991
bronze
cast no.2 from an edition of 6
plus 1 artist's cast
81 ½ × 12 ¾ × 16 ½ in / 207 × 32·4 × 41·9 cm

stamped with the artist's monogram,
inscribed with cast and edition number
"2/6" and date "91" on base

Provenance
The artist

Exhibited
'Sculpture', Waddington Galleries, London,
29 April–30 May 1992 (not repro. in
catalogue) (1/6 exhibited)
'William Turnbull', Galeria Freites, Caracas,
18 October–10 November 1992 (repro. in
colour in catalogue p.28)
'William Turnbull: Skulpturen', Galerie
Thomas, Munich, 5 April–19 June 2002
(not repro. in catalogue) (2/6 exhibited)
'The Secret Garden: An Exhibition of
Sculpture', The Solomon Gallery at
Iveagh Gardens, Dublin, 15–27 May 2008
(5/6 exhibited)

Literature
William Turnbull, Waddington Galleries,
London, 2004 (repro. in colour p.[33])
The Sculpture of William Turnbull, Amanda
A. Davidson, The Henry Moore Foundation
in association with Lund Humphries,
2005, catalogue no.277, p.181 (repro. in
b&w p.181)

22
Paddle Venus 3
1986
bronze
cast no.5 from an edition of 6
plus 1 artist's cast
73 ¼ × 14 ¼ × 19 ½ in / 186 × 36·2 × 49·5 cm
on bronze base

inscribed with the artist's monogram, cast
and edition number "5/6" and date "86" at
base, behind figure

Provenance
The artist

Literature
The Sculpture of William Turnbull, Amanda
A. Davidson, The Henry Moore Foundation
in association with Lund Humphries,
2005, catalogue no.247, p.170 (repro. in
b&w p.170)

23
Large Metamorphic Venus
1982
bronze
cast no.3 from an edition of 6
plus 1 artist's cast
68 ¾ × 31 × 10 in / 174·6 × 78·7 × 25·4 cm
on bronze base

stamped with the artist's monogram,
inscribed with cast and edition number
"3/6" and date "82" at base

Provenance
The artist

Exhibited
'Looking Forward: Thirty Contemporary
British Artists', Agnew's, London, 6 June–
21 July 2007 (repro. in colour in catalogue)
(4/6 exhibited)

Literature
The Sculpture of William Turnbull, Amanda
A. Davidson, The Henry Moore Foundation
in association with Lund Humphries,
2005, catalogue no.221, p.160 (repro. in
b&w p.160)

24
Horse 5
1988
bronze
cast no.1 from an edition of 6
plus 1 artist's cast
28 ¾ × 37 ¼ × 13 ⅛ in / 73 × 94·6 × 33·3 cm
on York stone base

stamped with the artist's monogram,
inscribed with cast and edition number
"1/6" and date "88" at base of neck

Provenance
The artist

Exhibited
'William Turnbull–Recent Sculpture', John
 Berggruen Gallery, San Francisco, 3
 November 1988–7 January 1989
'Post War Sculpture', Arnold Herstand &
 Company, New York, 14 July–September
 1989 (2/6 exhibited)
'William Turnbull: Recent Sculpture', Arnold
 Herstand & Company, New York, 19
 October–22 November 1989 (repro. in
 colour on announcement card) (2/6
 exhibited)
'William Turnbull: Recent Sculpture',
 Waddington Galleries, London, 25
 September–19 October 1991, catalogue
 no.3 (repro. in colour p.11) (4/6 exhibited)
'William Turnbull', Galeria Freites, Caracas,
 18 October–10 November 1992 (repro. in
 colour in catalogue p.18) (4/6 exhibited)
'William Turnbull: Skulpturen (1979–1991)',
 Galerie Sander, Darmstadt, 8 April–21
 May 1994 (1/6 exhibited)
'William Turnbull: Horses–Development of a
 Theme, Other Sculptures and Paintings',
 Waddington Galleries, London, 22 June–20
 July 2001, catalogue no.5 (repro. in colour
 p.[13]) (6/6 exhibited)
'William Turnbull: Sculpture', Barbara
 Mathes Gallery, New York, 26 April–28
 June 2002 (1/6 exhibited)
'Do Not Feed: Animals in Art', Galerie
 Thomas, Munich, 23 November 2006–27
 January 2007 (1/6 exhibited)

Literature
'William Turnbull: A Consistent Way of
 Thinking', Patrick Elliott, in *William
 Turnbull: sculpture and paintings*, David
 Sylvester (intro.), Merrell Holberton
 Publishers, in association with
 Serpentine Gallery, London, 1995, p.74
 (not repro.)
The Sculpture of William Turnbull, Amanda
 A. Davidson, The Henry Moore Foundation
 in association with Lund Humphries,
 2005, catalogue no.256, p.174 (repro. in
 b&w p.174)

25
Horse
1999
bronze
cast no.1 from an edition of 6
plus 1 artist's cast
71 ½ × 29 × 80 ¾ in / 181·5 × 73·6 × 205·1 cm

stamped with the artist's monogram, cast
and edition number "1/6" and date "99" at
base of neck

Provenance
The artist
Waddington Galleries, London
Private Collection, London

Exhibited
'William Turnbull: Horses–Development of a
 Theme, Other Sculptures and Paintings',
 Waddington Galleries, London, 22 June–
 20 July 2001, catalogue no.8 (repro. in
 colour p.[19]) (3/6 exhibited)

Literature
The Sculpture of William Turnbull, Amanda
 A. Davidson, The Henry Moore Foundation
 in association with Lund Humphries,
 2005, catalogue no.301, pp.[72] & 190
 (repro. in b&w p.190)

26
Large Horse
1990
bronze
cast no.2 from an edition of 5
plus 1 artist's cast
115 × 139 × 54 ½ in / 292 × 353 × 138·4 cm

stamped with the artist's monogram,
inscribed with cast and edition number
"2/5" and date "90" at base of neck

Provenance
The artist

Exhibited
'William Turnbull: Recent Sculpture',
    Waddington Galleries, London, 25
    September–19 October 1991, catalogue
    no.18 (repro. in colour p.41) (1/5 exhibited
    at The Economist Plaza, St. James's,
    London)
'Here & Now', Serpentine Gallery, London,
    19 June–2 July 1995 (repro. in b&w in
    exhibition brochure) (1/5 exhibited)
'British Sculpture', Schlosspark Ambras,
    Innsbruck, Austria, organised by Galerie
    Elisabeth and Klaus Thoman, Innsbruck,
    in collaboration with the Yorkshire
    Sculpture Park, West Bretton, Wakefield,
    27 June 1998–30 September 1999, no.24
    (repro. in colour in exhibition brochure)
    (1/5 exhibited)
'William Turnbull: Horses–Development of a
    Theme, Other Sculptures and Paintings',
    Waddington Galleries, London, 22 June–20
    July 2001, catalogue no.6 (repro. in colour
    p.[15]) (1/5 exhibited at Yorkshire
    Sculpture Park)
'William Turnbull: Retrospective 1946–2003',
    Yorkshire Sculpture Park, West Bretton,
    Wakefield, 14 May–9 October 2005
    (exhibition guide p.17, repro. in colour
    p.[19], fig.32) (2/5 exhibited)

Literature
William Turnbull, Waddington Galleries,
    London, 2004 (repro. in colour pp.[30–31])

The Sculpture of William Turnbull, Amanda
    A. Davidson, The Henry Moore Foundation
    in association with Lund Humphries,
    2005, catalogue no.276, pp.23, [72] & 180
    (repro. in b&w p.180)
Sculpture, Waddington Galleries, London,
    2007, no.33 (repro. in colour p.67) (2/5
    catalogued)
Yorkshire Sculpture Park: Landscape for Art,
    Lynne Green (et al.), Yorkshire Sculpture
    Park, West Bretton, Wakefield, 2008
    (repro. in colour p.[296])

27
Untitled
1957
oil on canvas
60 × 45 in / 152·4 × 114·3 cm

signed and dated on reverse and overlap
"Turnbull 1957"

Provenance
The artist

28
Untitled
1957
oil on canvas
60 × 45 in / 152·4 × 114·3 cm

signed and dated on reverse
"Turnbull 1957"

Provenance
The artist

29
Untitled
1957
oil on canvas
60 × 45 in / 152·4 × 114·3 cm

signed and dated on reverse
"Turnbull 1957"

Provenance
The artist

30
24–1958
oil on canvas
78 × 58 in / 198·1 × 147·3 cm

signed and dated on reverse "Turnbull
1958"; titled and signed on overlap
"24–1958" "Turnbull"

Provenance
The artist

31
23–1958
oil on canvas
78 × 58 in / 198·1 × 147·3 cm

signed and dated on reverse "Turnbull
1958"; titled on overlap "23–1958"

Provenance
The artist

32
9–1959
oil on canvas
70 × 70 in / 177·8 × 177·8 cm

signed and titled on overlap "Turnbull"
"9–1959"

Provenance
The artist

33
5–1959
oil on canvas
60 × 60 in / 152·4 × 152·4 cm

signed and dated on reverse "Turnbull
59"; titled and signed on overlap "5–1959"
"Turnbull"; also inscribed "TOURNAMENT"
and "YIN + YANG"

Provenance
The artist

34
12–1960
oil on canvas
72 × 60 in / 183 × 152·4 cm

signed and titled on overlap "Turnbull"
"12–60"; also inscribed "EXPANDING RED"

Provenance
The artist

BIOGRAPHY

1922 Born Dundee, Scotland, 11 January

1937 After leaving school he takes odd jobs as a labourer, and attends art classes two or three evenings a week at Dundee University where he is taught by the landscape painter James McIntosh Patrick

1939–41 Employed in the illustration department of D.C. Thompson, a national periodical company in Dundee, where he works alongside a number of designers and illustrators

1941 Drafted into the Services, he joins the RAF as a pilot, and flies on war service in Canada, India and Ceylon

1946 Accepted into the painting department at the Slade School of Fine Art, London, but almost immediately transfers to the sculpture department

1947 Spends six weeks travelling in Italy, and on the way back visits Paris for the first time

1948 Moves to Paris where he meets Léger, Giacometti and Brancusi among others

1950 In February, he has a joint exhibition with Eduardo Paolozzi at the Hanover Gallery, London, organized by a mutual friend David Sylvester. At the end of the year, takes up permanent residence in London. Makes two films with Alan Forbes, an American living in London, which are later shown at the Institute of Contemporary Arts (ICA)

1952 Included in 'Young Sculptors' at the Institute of Contemporary Arts (ICA), the focal point for new art in London. Becomes a member of the Independent Group, a splinter group within the ICA which became an important forum for discussion and debate. Included in 'New Aspects of British Sculpture', an exhibition in the British Pavilion at the Venice Biennale selected by Herbert Read. Teaches experimental design at the Central School of Arts and Crafts, London, a part-time position he holds until 1961

1955 Makes his first standing figure, a subject that represents a new preoccupation with stillness and silence

1957 Abandons figurative references in his painting. Visits the USA for the first time and travels to New York where he is introduced to Mark Rothko and Barnett Newman by Donald Blinken

1960 Marries sculptor and printmaker, Kim Lim. They have two sons, Alex and Johnny

1962–63 First visits to Japan, Cambodia, and Lim's native Singapore. A series of gate sculptures followed, inspired by the religious sites he had visited on his recent travels

1964 Teaches sculpture part-time at the Central School of Arts and Crafts, a position he holds until 1972. Begins working in steel, a medium he continues to explore over the next eight years or so

1967–68 Works in Perspex and fibreglass, materials he values for their reflective quality and their transparency

1969 Designs *Basho: The Records of a Weathered Exposed Skeleton*, a book of haiku poetry by the seventeenth-century Japanese writer Matsuo Basho, published in a limited edition by Alistair McAlpine Publishing Ltd, London

1970 Makes a series of drawings to illustrate *The Garden of Caresses*, an anonymous Arabian text from around the tenth century A.D., published in a limited edition by Alistair McAlpine Publishing Ltd, London

1972 Commissioned by the Peter Stuyvesant Foundation to create a public sculpture for the Peter Stuyvesant City Sculpture Project, for which eight cities were asked to show sculptures by two artists for six months. Turnbull was invited to show in Liverpool

1973 Major retrospective exhibition opens at the Tate Gallery, organized by Richard Morphet. On seeing all his work together in one exhibition, Turnbull decides to re-think the direction of his work. He begins to move away from the more modular, steel sculptures he had been creating and returns to the moulded, textured work of his early career

1982 Included in the second part of a major survey of British sculpture in the 20th century, 'Symbol and Imagination 1951–1980', at the Whitechapel Art Gallery

1984 Joint exhibition with Kim Lim at the National Museum Art Gallery, Singapore

1987 Included in 'British Art in the Twentieth Century: The Modern Movement' at the Royal Academy of Arts, London touring to Staatsgalerie Stuttgart

1995 An exhibition of sculpture and paintings, selected by David Sylvester, opens at the Serpentine Gallery in November

1998 Exhibition of sculpture and paintings opens at Waddington Galleries in June

2001 'Horses – Development of a theme, Other Sculptures and Paintings' opens at Waddington Galleries in June

2004 *Large Horse*, 1990, installed at Yorkshire Sculpture Park, Wakefield. Exhibition of paintings and bronze sculpture opens at Waddington Galleries in November

2005 Major exhibition, 'William Turnbull: Retrospective 1946–2003', opens at Yorkshire Sculpture Park, Wakefield in May

2006 Survey exhibition of sculpture opens at Tate Britain's Duveen Galleries in June

2007 Exhibition of sculpture and paintings opens at Waddington Galleries in January

Lives and works in London

SOLO EXHIBITIONS

1950 Hanover Gallery, London (sculpture)

1952 Hanover Gallery, London (sculpture and paintings)

1957 Institute of Contemporary Arts, London (sculpture and paintings)

1960 Molton Gallery, London (sculpture)

1961 Molton Gallery, London (paintings)

1963 Marlborough-Gerson Gallery, New York (sculpture)
Art Institute, Detroit (sculpture)

1965 Bennington College, Vermont (paintings)
Galerie Müller, Stuttgart (paintings)

1966 Pavilion Gallery, Balboa, California (sculpture and paintings)

1967 Waddington Galleries, London (sculpture and paintings)

1967–68 IX Bienal, São Paulo; touring to Museo de Arte Moderna, Rio de Janeiro; Museo National de Belles Artes, Buenos Aires; Institute de Artes Plasticas, Santiago (sculpture and paintings)

1968 Hayward Gallery, London (paintings)

1969 Waddington Galleries, London (lithographs)

1970 Waddington Galleries, London (sculpture and paintings)

1973 Tate Gallery, London (sculpture and paintings retrospective)

1974 Scottish Arts Council, Edinburgh (sculpture, paintings and prints)
Galerie Müller, Stuttgart (paintings)

1976 Waddington Galleries, London (paintings and prints)

1978 Waddington and Tooth Galleries, London (drawings)

1981 Waddington Galleries, London (sculpture)
The Scottish Gallery, Edinburgh (sculpture)

1982 Waddington & Shiell Fine Art, Toronto, and Theo Waddington Fine Arts, New York (sculpture)

1983 Galerie Kutter, Luxembourg (sculpture)

1984 National Museum Art Gallery, Singapore (sculpture, with Kim Lim)

1985 Waddington Galleries, London (sculpture)

1986 Terry Dintenfass Inc., New York (sculpture)

1987 Galerie Folker Skulima, Berlin (sculpture)
Waddington Galleries, London (sculpture retrospective)

1988 Terry Dintenfass Inc., New York (sculpture)

1988–89 John Berggruen Gallery, San Francisco (sculpture)

1989 Arnold Herstand & Company, New York (sculpture and drawings)

1990 Jesus College, Cambridge (sculpture)

1991 Waddington Galleries and The Economist Plaza, London (sculpture)

1992 Galeria Freites, Caracas (sculpture)
Galerie Michael Haas, Berlin (sculpture)
Galerie von Braunbehrens, Munich (sculpture)

1994 Galerie Sander, Darmstadt (sculpture)

1995–96 Serpentine Gallery, London
(sculpture and paintings retrospective)

1998 Waddington Galleries, London
(sculpture and paintings)
Barbara Mathes Gallery, New York
(sculpture)

2001 Waddington Galleries, London
(sculpture and paintings)

2002 Galerie Thomas, Munich (sculpture)
Barbara Mathes Gallery, New York
(sculpture)

2004 James Hyman Fine Art, London (works
on paper)
Waddington Galleries, London (sculpture
and paintings)

2005 Yorkshire Sculpture Park, Wakefield
(sculpture, paintings and works on paper)

2006 Duveen Galleries, Tate Britain, London
(sculpture)

2007 Waddington Galleries, London
(sculpture and paintings)

SELECTED GROUP EXHIBITIONS

1950 *Les mains éblouis*, Galerie Maeght,
Paris
Aspects of British Art, Institute of
Contemporary Arts, London

1951 *Abstract Art*, Riverside Museum, New
York

1952 *XXVI Biennale*, British Pavilion, Venice
Young Sculptors, Institute of Contemporary
Arts, London

1956 *Contemporary Sculpture*, Hanover
Gallery, London
This is Tomorrow, Whitechapel Art Gallery,
London

1956–57 *Y ngre Brittiska Skulptorer*,
Gothenburg Museum; touring to
Sandviken; Linköping; Tranås; Lund;
Halsingborg; Halmstad; Falkenberg;
Örebro; Stockholm

1957 *Dimensions*, O'Hana Gallery, London
Ten British Sculptors Exhibition, Biennale
São Paulo; touring to Rio de Janeiro;
Buenos Aires; Montevideo; Santiago;
Lima; Caracas

1958 *Contemporary British Sculpture*, Arts
Council of Great Britain, London; touring
to Japson Gardens, Leamington Spa;
Shrewsbury Castle; Bute Park, Cardiff
Exploration of Form, Tooth Gallery, London
New Trends in British Art, New York–Rome
Art Foundation, Rome
Carnegie International, Museum of Art,
Carnegie Institute, Pittsburgh,
Pennsylvania

1959 *Biennale*, Middleheim, Antwerp
Bronzetti, Biennale d'Arte Triveneta, Padua

1959–60 *European Art Today: 35 Painters and Sculptors*, Minneapolis Institute of Arts; touring to Los Angeles County Museum; San Francisco Museum of Art; North Carolina Museum of Art; National Gallery of Canada, Ottawa; French & Co., New York; Baltimore Museum of Art

1960 *Situation*, R.B.A. Galleries, London
The Mysterious Sign, Institute of Contemporary Arts, London
Sculpture in the Open Air, Battersea Park, London

1961 *Bronzetti*, Biennale d'Arte Triveneta, Padua
Ten Sculptors, Marlborough New London Gallery
New London Situation, Marlborough New London Gallery
2nd International Exhibition of Sculpture, Musée Rodin, Paris
Neue Malerei in England, Stadtisches Museum, Leverkusen, Germany
Carnegie International, Museum of Art, Carnegie Institute, Pittsburgh, Pennsylvania

1962 *Maestri de XIX/XX Secolo*, Marlborough Galleria d'Arte, Rome
Aspects of 20th Century Art, Marlborough Fine Art, London
Hoyland, Plumb, Stroud, Turnbull, Marlborough New London Gallery
Premio International de Escuoltura, Instituto di Tella, Buenos Aires
Mostra Internazionale de Scultura, Galleria Toninelli, Spoleto, Italy
Hirshhorn Collection, Solomon R. Guggenheim Museum, New York
British Art Today, San Francisco Museum of Art; touring to Dallas Museum of Contemporary Art; Santa Barbara Museum of Art; Museum of Art, Carnegie Institute, Pittsburgh, Pennsylvania

1963 *Junge Englische Maler*, Kunsthalle, Basel
7th International Art Exhibition, Tokyo

Sculpture in the Open Air, Battersea Park, London
IV Biennale Internazionale d'Arte, San Marino

1964 *Contemporary British Painting and Sculpture*, Albright-Knox Art Gallery, Buffalo, New York
International Graphics, Albright-Knox Art Gallery, Buffalo, New York
Profile III, Englische Kunst der Gegenwart, Stadtisches Kunstmuseum Bochum, Germany
Guggenheim International, Solomon R. Guggenheim Museum, New York
Painting and Sculpture of a Decade, Tate Gallery, London

1965 *British Sculpture in the Sixties*, Tate Gallery, London
Signale, Kunsthalle, Basel
Drawings from the Betty Parsons Collection, New York
Sculpture from the Albert A. List Family Collection, New School Art Center, New York

1966 *Sculpture in the Open Air*, Battersea Park, London
Sonsbeek Park, Arnhem
New Shapes and Forms of Colour, Stedelijk Museum, Amsterdam

1967 *Formen der Farbe*, Württembergischer Kunstverein, Stuttgart; touring to Kunsthalle, Bern
Guggenheim International, Solomon R. Guggenheim Museum, New York

1968 *Documenta 4*, Kassel, Germany
Sculpture in the City, Arts Council Gallery, London; touring to Post & Mail Building, Birmingham; Goree Piazza, Liverpool; Southampton Civic Centre

1969 *Biennale*, Middleheim, Antwerp
First International Exhibition of Modern Sculpture, Hakone Open Air Museum, Japan

1971 *The Alistair McAlpine Gift*, Tate Gallery, London

1972 *20th Century Sculpture in Los Angeles Collections*, U.C.L.A. Galleries, Los Angeles

1974 *Kunstler machen Fahnen fur Rottweil*, Stadtfest Rottweil, Germany
British Painting, Hayward Gallery, London
Artistas Graficos Britanicos de la Decade del 60, British Council exhibition; touring to Rio de Janeiro, Recife, Belo Horizonte, Brazilia, Sao Paulo, Curitiba, Porto Alegre, Mar del Plata, Rosario, Cordoba, Buenos Aires, Lima, Bogota, Medelin, Cali, Barranquila

1975 *The Need to Draw*, Scottish Arts Council Gallery, Edinburgh; touring to Aberdeen Art Gallery; Dundee City Art Gallery

1976 *Arte Inglese Oggi*, Palazzo Reale, Milan
The Human Clay, Hayward Gallery, London

1977 *Hayward Annual*, Hayward Gallery, London
Silver Jubilee Exhibition of British Sculpture, Battersea Park, London
Color en la Pintura Britanica, British Council exhibition; touring to Rio de Janeiro, Brazilia, Curitiba, São Paulo, Buenos Aires, Caracas, Bogota, Mexico City
Drawings and Watercolours of Distinction, Victor Waddington Gallery, London
Private Images (photographs by sculptors), Los Angeles County Museum of Art
British Painting 1952–77, Royal Academy of Arts, London

1977–78 *Series*, Tate Gallery, London
Carved-Modelled-Constructed, Tate Gallery, London

1978 *Groups*, Waddington & Tooth Galleries, London

The Mechanised Image, Arts Council of Great Britain exhibition; touring to Portsmouth; Sheffield; London; Kingston-upon-Hull; Newcastle upon Tyne; Aberdeen
The Museum of Drawers, Cooper-Hewitt Museum, New York; touring to Kunsthaus, Zurich
John Moores Liverpool Exhibition, Walker Art Gallery, Liverpool (2nd prize)

1979 *Sculpture Européenne*, Château Malou, Brussels
Groups II, Waddington Galleries, London
Tate 79 (inaugural exhibition for the new extension), Tate Gallery, London

1980 *Groups III*, Waddington Galleries, London

1981 *Sculpture for the Blind*, Tate Gallery, London
Artists in Camden, Camden Arts Centre, London

1981–82 *British Sculpture in the Twentieth century: Part 1: Image and Form 1901–1950 | Part 2: Symbol and Imagination 1951–1980*, Whitechapel Art Gallery, London

1982 *A Selection from the permanent collection of prints*, Tate Gallery, London
Sculpture, Waddington Galleries, London

1983–84 *Views and Horizons*, Yorkshire Sculpture Park, Wakefield
Drawing in Air, an Exhibition of Sculptors Drawings 1882–1982, Sunderland Arts Centre exhibition, Ceolfrith Gallery, Sunderland; touring to Glynn Vivian Art Gallery & Museum, Swansea; City Art Gallery and Henry Moore Study Centre, Leeds

1985 *Sculptors' Drawings*, Scottish Arts Council Gallery, Edinburgh
Hands, Anne Berthoud Gallery, London
Twenty-Five Years, Annely Juda/Juda Rowan Gallery, London

Malerei Plastik Objekt, Museum Morsbroich, Leverkusen, Germany

1986 *Forty Years of Modern Art 1945–1985*, Tate Gallery, London
British Sculpture 1950–1965, New Art Centre, London
From Figuration to Abstraction, Annely Juda Fine Art, London
Sculpture and Works in Relief, John Berggruen Gallery, San Francisco
Trends in Geometric Abstract Art: The Riklis Collection of the McCrory Corporation, Tel Aviv Museum, Israel

1987 *British Art in the Twentieth Century: The Modern Movement*, Royal Academy of Arts, London; touring to Staatsgalerie, Stuttgart
Ancient & Modern, McAlpine Gallery, Ashmolean Museum, Oxford
Forty Years of British Sculpture, National Gallery and Alexander Soutzos Museum, Athens

1988 *Abstract Art From Sheffield's Collection*, Mappin Art Gallery, Sheffield
Sculpture, Waddington Galleries, London
Britannica: Trente Ans de Sculpture, Musée des Beaux-Arts, Le Havre; touring to Musée de l'Evêché, Evreux; Ecole d'Architecture de Normandie, Rouen; Museum Van Hedendaagse Kunst, Antwerp (here re-titled 'British Sculpture 1960–1988'); Centre Régional d'Art Contemporain, Toulouse
Glasgow Garden Festival, Glasgow
Minimalistische Tendenzen Sammlung Sybil Albers, Stiftung fur Konstruktive und Konkrete Kunst, Zurich
Modern British Sculpture from the Collection, Tate Gallery, Liverpool

1988–89 *Sculpteurs Anglais du XXième Siècle*, Artcurial, Paris

1989 *The London Opening*, Scottish Gallery, London
From Picasso to Abstraction, Annely Juda Fine Art, London

Post War Sculpture, Arnold Herstand & Company, New York
Scottish Art Since 1900, Scottish National Gallery of Modern Art, Edinburgh; touring to Barbican Art Gallery, London
Aus der Sammlung Sybil Albers-Barrier, Stiftung fur Konstruktive und Konkrete Kunst, Zurich

1989–90 *From Prism to Paintbox: Colour Theory and Practice in British Painting*, Oriel Gallery, Clwyd; touring to Warrington Museum & Art Gallery; Cooper Art Gallery, Barnsley

1990 *Studies on Paper, Contemporary British Sculptors*, Connaught Brown, London
20th Century Scottish Drawings, Scottish Gallery, Edinburgh
164th Annual Exhibition 1990, Royal Scottish Academy, Edinburgh (guest artist)
New Hanging, Tate Gallery, London
Hands, Grob Gallery, London
For the Collector: Important 20th Century Sculpture, Meredith Long & Company, Houston, Texas

1990–91 *The Independent Group: Postwar Britain and the Aesthetics of Plenty*, Institute of Contemporary Arts, London; touring to IVAM Centro Julio Gonzalez, Valencia; Museum of Contemporary Art, Los Angeles; University Art Museum, University of California at Berkeley; Hood Museum of Art, Dartmouth College, Hanover, New Hampshire

1991 *British Art from 1930*, Waddington Galleries, London
Avant-Garde British Printmaking 1914–60, The British Museum, London
New Displays 1991, Tate Gallery, London
Virtue and Vision: Sculpture and Scotland 1540–1990, Royal Scottish Academy, Edinburgh
Saved for Scotland, National Gallery of Scotland, Edinburgh
Sculpture Garden at Roche Court, New Art Centre, Wiltshire

Sculpture by the Spire | Salisbury Festival, Salisbury Cathedral Close and Courcoux & Courcoux Gallery, Salisbury

1992 *4 Sculpteurs Anglais: Armitage, Caro, Chadwick, Turnbull*, Artcurial, Paris
Ready, Steady, Go: Painting of the Sixties from the Arts Council Collection, Royal Festival Hall, South Bank Centre, London; touring Britain
Sculpture, Waddington Galleries, London
New Realities, Art in Western Europe 1945–68, Tate Gallery, Liverpool
Le Cri et la Raison, L'espace de l'art concret, Château de Mouans, Sartoux, Côtes d'Azur
New Beginnings: Postwar British Art from the collection of Ken Powell, Scottish National Gallery of Modern Art, Edinburgh; touring to Graves Art Gallery, Sheffield

1993 *A Sculptor's Landscape*, New Art Centre, London
Sculpture Garden at Roche Court, New Art Centre, Wiltshire
Works from the Collection, Yorkshire Sculpture Park, Wakefield
The Sixties Art Scene in London, Barbican Art Gallery, London

1994 *Sculpture Garden at Roche Court*, New Art Centre, Wiltshire
Back to the Future: Contemporary British Sculpture at Arundel Great Court, curated for Andersen Consulting by Art Guidelines Ltd
Tresors Fair, Singapore

1995 *Sculpture Garden at Roche Court*, New Art Centre, Wiltshire
Here and Now, Serpentine Gallery, London
British Abstract Art Part 2: Sculpture, Flowers East, London
Of the Human Form, Waddington Galleries, London

1996 *un siècle de sculpture anglaise*, galerie nationale du Jeu de Paume, Paris

British Abstract Art Part 3: Works on Paper, Flowers East, London
Mostly Monochrome, Green on Red Gallery, Dublin
Sculpture in the Close, Jesus College, Cambridge

1997 *From Blast to Pop: Aspects of Modern British Art, 1915–1965*, David and Alfred Smart Museum of Art, University of Chicago
Surrealism and After: The Gabrielle Keiller Collection, Scottish National Gallery of Modern Art, Edinburgh

1998 *British Figurative Art: Part Two: Sculpture*, Flowers East, London

1998–99 *Transistors: New Small Sculpture from Scotland*, organised by the Iwate Art Festival UK98, Morioka Hashimoto Museum of Art, Japan; touring to the Royal Scottish Museum of Scotland, Edinburgh

1999 *Colour Sculptures: Britain in the Sixties*, Waddington Galleries, London
British Sculpture, Schloss Ambras, Innsbruck, Austria

2000 *Welded Sculpture of the Twentieth Century*, Neuberger Museum of Art, Purchase, New York

2001–02 *Close Encounters: The Sculptor's Studio in the Age of the Camera*, Henry Moore Institute, Leeds

2002 *Transition: The London Art Scene in the Fifties*, Barbican Art Gallery, London
United Kingdom United States, Waddington Galleries, London
Henry Moore and the Geometry of Fear, James Hyman Fine Art, London

2002–03 *Blast to Freeze: British Art in the 20th Century*, Kunstmuseum Wolfsburg, Germany; touring to Les Abattoirs, Toulouse

2003 *Pour l'amour de Vénus*, Donjon de Vez, Vez, France

2004 *The challenge of post-war painting*, James Hyman Fine Art, London

2004–05 *Art and the 60s: This Was Tomorrow*, Tate Britain, London; touring to Gas Hall, Birmingham Museums and Art Gallery

2005 *40 Jahre Galerie Thomas, Nr 2*, Galerie Thomas, Munich

2006 *Please close the gate: painted sculpture at Roche Court*, New Art Centre, Roche Court, Wiltshire

2007 *Circa 1967: Works from the Arts Council Collection*, Milton Keynes Gallery
A Tribute to Sir Colin St John Wilson, James Hyman Gallery, London
Looking Forward: Thirty Contemporary British Artists, Agnew's, London

2008 *The Secret Garden*, The Solomon Gallery at Iveagh Gardens, Dublin

PUBLIC COLLECTIONS

Albright-Knox Art Gallery, Buffalo, New York
Arts Council Collection, Hayward Gallery, London
Art Gallery of Ontario, Toronto
British Council, London
Contemporary Art Society, London
David and Alfred Smart Museum of Art, University of Chicago
Dundee Museum and Art Gallery
Franklin P. Murphy Sculpture Garden, U.C.L.A., Los Angeles
Glasgow Museum and Art Gallery
The Government Art Collection, London (Department for Culture, Media and Sport)
Hirshhorn Museum and Sculpture Garden, Smithsonian Institution, Washington D.C.
Hull University Art Collection, Kingston-upon-Hull
Hunterian Art Gallery, University of Glasgow
McCrory Corporation, New York
Museum of Contemporary Art, Tehran
National Gallery of Art, Washington D.C.
Scottish National Gallery of Modern Art, Edinburgh
Sintra Museum of Modern Art, Portugal - The Berardo Collection
Städtisches Museum, Leverkusen, Germany
Swindon Museum and Art Gallery
Sydney Opera House
Tate, London
Victoria and Albert Museum, London
Westfälisches Landesmuseum, Münster, Germany

SELECTED BIBLIOGRAPHY

1950 Sylvester, David (intro.): *William Turnbull* (catalogue), Hanover Gallery, London

1952 Banham, Reyner: 'The Next Step', *Art News and Review*, 26 January
Ritchie, Andrew C.: *Sculpture of the Twentieth Century* (catalogue), Museum of Modern Art, New York

1953 Waldberg, Isabelle: 'Essor de la Sculpture Anglaise', *Numero*, vol.5, nos.1 & 2, January/March
Alloway, Lawrence: 'Britain's New Iron Age', *ARTnews*, vol.52, June, pp.18–20 & 68–70

1957 Alloway, Lawrence: 'Sculpture as Walls and Playgrounds', *Architectural Design* 27, January, p.26
Forge, Andrew: 'Round the London Galleries', *The Listener*, 10 October, p.547
Butcher, G.M: 'Alchemist Priest', *Art News and Review*, 12 October, p.10
Alloway, Lawrence (intro.): 'A Note on William Turnbull's Technique', *William Turnbull* (catalogue), Institute of Contemporary Arts, London

1958 Alloway, Lawrence: 'Marks and Signs', *Ark*, no.22, pp.37–41

1959 Seuphor, Michel: 'Le Choix d'un Critique', *L'Oeil*, no.49, p.31
Alloway, Lawrence (intro.): *European Art Today* (catalogue), Walker Art Center, Minneapolis

1960 Coleman, Roger: 'William Turnbull', *Art News and Review*, 13 August
Alloway, Lawrence: 'Avant Garde, London', *Image*, October
Seuphor, Michel: *The Sculpture of this Century*, Wittenbourne, New York
Geidion-Welcker, Carola: *Contemporary Sculpture*, Wittenbourne, New York

Alloway, Lawrence (intro.): 'Aphoristics and Monumental', *William Turnbull* (catalogue), Molton Gallery, London
Coleman, Roger (intro.): *Situation* (catalogue), R.B.A. Galleries, London

1961 Alloway, Lawrence: 'The Sculpture and Painting of William Turnbull', *Art International,* vol.5, no.1, 1 February, pp.46–52
Reichardt, Jasia: 'Bill Turnbull', *Art News and Review*, 22 April
'In Brancusi's Vein', *The Times*, 3 May
Langsner, Jules: 'The Way I See It', *California*, 11 May
Crosby, Theo: 'International Union of Architects Congress Building, South Bank', (statement by William Turnbull), *Architectural Design*, November, pp.484–509
Alloway, Lawrence (intro.): 'Sculpture', *William Turnbull* (catalogue), Molton Gallery, London
Kulterman, Udo: *Neue Malerei in England* (catalogue), Stadtisches Museum, Leverkusen, Germany

1962 Renfrew, Colin: 'The Tyranny of the Renaissance', *Cambridge Review*, 27 January, pp.219–223
Kulterman, Udo: *Speculum Artis* (Zurich), January/February
'LCC patronage of the arts', *Art and Design*, vol.XXXII, February
Kulterman, Udo: 'Neue Malerei in England', *Das Kunstwerk*, May, pp.2–9
Arnason, H. H. (intro.): *Modern Sculpture in the Joseph H. Hirshhorn Collection* (catalogue), Solomon R. Guggenheim Museum, New York, pp.58–59

1963 Hakanson, Joy: 'British Artist's Massive Sculptures Shown Here', *Detroit News*, December
Driver, Morley: 'The Panorama of Centuries', *Art in Detroit*, December
Turnbull (catalogue), Marlborough Gerson Gallery, New York

1964 Thieman, Eugen: 'William Turnbull', *Das Kunstwerk*, no.8/xvii, February, pp.7–23

Alloway, Lawrence (intro.): *Guggenheim International* (catalogue), Solomon R. Guggenheim Museum, New York

Read, Herbert: *A Concise History of Modern Sculpture*, Thames & Hudson, London

International Directory of Contemporary Art, Editoriale Metro, Milan

Painting & Sculpture of a Decade (catalogue), Tate Gallery, London

1965 Rudlinger, Arnold: *Signale* (catalogue), Kunsthalle, Basel

Baro, Gene (intro.): 'Paintings', *William Turnbull* (catalogue), Bennington College, Vermont

1966 Baro, Gene: 'A Changed Englishman, William Turnbull', *Art in America*, vol.54, March/April, pp.102–103

Baro, Gene: 'Turnbull's Nudes', *London Magazine*, September, pp.39–43

Baro, Gene: 'British Sculpture: The Developing Scene', *Studio International*, October, pp.171–182

Langsner, Jules (intro.): *William Turnbull* (catalogue), Pavilion Gallery, Balboa, California

1967 Russell, J.: 'Down to the Bones', *The Sunday Times*, 16 April

Wolfram, E.: 'Profile of Turnbull', *Art News and Review*, April, p.113

Huberman, B.: 'La Aventura Artistica de William Turnbull', *La Voz del Interior* (Buenos Aires)

Whitford, Frank: 'The Paintings of William Turnbull', *Studio*, April, pp.202–204

Reichhardt, Jasia: 'William Turnbull', *Architectural Design*, May, p.205

Bowness, Alan: 'William Turnbull', *IX Bienal Sao Paulo* (catalogue), British Council

William Turnbull: Sculpture and Paintings (catalogue), The Waddington Galleries, London

1968 *Sculpture 1967–68* (catalogue), Waddington Galleries, London

1970 Lynton, Norbert: 'Waddington: Minimal Art', *The Guardian*, 25 March

1971 Morphet, Richard: 'William Turnbull', *Alistair McAlpine Gift* (catalogue), Tate Gallery, London, pp.106–121

1972 *Tate Gallery Acquisitions 1970–72*, Tate Gallery Publications, London, pp.197–198

1973 Cohen, Bernard: 'William Turnbull – Painter and Sculptor', *Studio International*, vol.186, July/August, pp.9–16

Oille, Jennifer: 'William Turnbull', *Arts Review*, vol.XXV, no.17, August

McNay, Michael: 'More or Less', *Manchester Guardian*, 18 August

Gaunt, William: 'William Turnbull', *The Times*, 22 August

Shepherd, Michael: 'Matter of Form', *The Sunday Telegraph*, 9 September

Hilton, Tim: 'The Scot who went to Paris', *The Observer*, 9 September

Whitford, Frank: 'Presbyterianischer Zen', *Kunstforum*, October, pp.205–210

Morphet, Richard (intro.): *William Turnbull, Sculpture and Painting* (catalogue), Tate Gallery, London

1974 Feaver, William: 'William Turnbull', *Art International*, September, vol.XVIII, no.7, pp.28–32

Morphet, Richard (intro.): *Recent Paintings, Sculptures and Prints by William Turnbull* (catalogue), Scottish Arts Council Gallery, Edinburgh

Kudielka, Robert (intro.): 'Bilder', *William Turnbull* (catalogue), Galerie Muller, Stuttgart

1976 Wight, Frederick S: *The Potent Image*, Macmillian, New York, pp.550–551

1977 Shone, Richard: *The Century of Change: British Painting Since 1900*, Phaidon Press, Oxford

1978 Burn, Guy: 'William Turnbull at Waddington & Tooth', *Art Review*, July

William Turnbull: Drawings (catalogue), Waddington & Tooth Galleries, London

1979 Cohen, Bernard: 'William Turnbull – Painter and Sculptor', *Decade* (Boston), February, pp.30–38
Wilson, Simon: *British Art*, Bodley Head, London

1981 Burr, James: 'Sculptural Intelligence', *Apollo*, March
Collier, Caroline: 'The Eternal Now', *Arts Review*, 13 March
Vaizey, Marina: 'William Turnbull', *The Sunday Times*, 15 March
Glaves-Smith, John: 'Turnbull', *Art Monthly*, no.45 , April
William Turnbull (catalogue), Waddington Galleries, London

1982 Kramer, Hilton: 'William Turnbull', *The New York Times*, 8 January
Duncan, Stephen: 'Tension and Vitality, Figuration: Sculpture of the Fifties', *Artscribe*, no.35, June, pp.50–53

1983 *William Turnbull* (catalogue), Galerie Kutter, Luxembourg

1984 Ngui, Caroline: 'Sculpture with a Presence', *The Straits Times*, 19 September
Yu, Grace: 'Of subtle bronzes and cool stones', *Business Times* (Singapore), 24 September
Bevan, Roger (intro.): *Kim Lim and William Turnbull* (catalogue), National Museum of Singapore
Strachan, W. J.: *Sutton Manor: permanent exhibition of XXth century sculpture*, Sutton Manor Arts Centre, Hampshire

1985 Johnstone, Mog: 'William Turnbull' (review), *Time Out*, 5–11 December
William Turnbull (catalogue), Waddington Galleries, London

1986 Gooding, Mel: 'William Turnbull; Jock McFayden, Julian Trevelyan', *Art Monthly*, no.93, pp.16–17

Johnstone, Mog: 'William Turnbull', *Artline*, vol.3, no.1, pp.16–17
Massey, Anne: 'Pop at the I.C.A.', *Art and Artists*, no.236, May, pp.11–14
Heartney, Eleanor: 'William Turnbull at Dintenfass', *Art in America*, May
H. S.: 'William Turnbull', *ARTnews*, New York

1987 Massey, Anne: 'The Independent Group: towards a redefinition', *Burlington Magazine*, vol.129, no.1009, pp.232–42
Beaumont, Mary Rose: 'William Turnbull', *Arts Review*, 6 November, p.766
Russell, John: 'William Turnbull', *The New York Times*, 17 November
Russell Taylor, John: 'Shape of Things to Come', *The Times*, 17 November
Garlake, Margaret: 'Turnbull, Kestelman, Hyslop, McAleer', *Art Monthly*, December/January 1988, pp.25–26
Bevan, Roger (intro.): *William Turnbull* (catalogue), Waddington Galleries, London

1988 Thomas, Mona: 'La sculpture anglaise', *Beaux Arts*, November, no.62, p.106
Curtis, Penelope: *Modern British Sculpture from the Collection*, Tate Gallery, Liverpool, pp.79 & 89–90
Ollier, Bridget: 'La Sculpture anglaise prend aimant en Normandie', *Libération*
Grenier, Catherine, Françoise Cohen and Lynne Cooke: *Britannica: Trente Ans de Sculpture* (catalogue), Centre Régional d'Art Contemporain Midi-Pyrénées

1989 Dobbels, Daniel: 'La Croisade des Anglais', *Libération*, 19 April
Wilson, Simon: *Tate Gallery: An Illustrated Companion*, Tate Gallery Publications, London
Curtis, Penelope: *Patronage & Practice: Sculpture on Merseyside*, Tate Gallery, Liverpool
Hartley, Keith: *Scottish Art since 1900* (catalogue), Scottish National Gallery of Modern Art, Edinburgh

1990 Morphet, Richard (intro.): *Sculpture in the Close* (catalogue), Jesus College, Cambridge

Renfrew, Colin: 'The Sculptures of William Turnbull', *Sculpture in the Close* (catalogue), Jesus College, Cambridge

Robbins, David: *The Independent Group: Postwar Britain and the Aesthetics of Plenty*, MIT Press, Cambridge, Massachusetts, and London

1991 Phelps, Edward: 'Sculpture by the Spire', *Arts Review,* vol.XLIII, no.19, 20 September, p.467

Searle, Adrian: 'William Turnbull; Waddington's', *Time Out*, 9–16 October

Pearson, Fiona (ed.): *Virtue and Vision, Sculpture and Scotland 1540–1990* (catalogue), National Galleries of Scotland

William Turnbull (catalogue), Waddington Galleries, London

Livingstone, Marco: *Pop Art* (catalogue), Royal Academy of Arts, London, p.147

1992 *Ready, Steady, Go: Painting of the Sixties from the Arts Council Collection* (catalogue), Arts Council and South Bank Centre, London

Sculpture (catalogue), Waddington Galleries, London

Le Cri et La Raison (catalogue), L'espace de l'art concret, Château de Mouans, Sartoux, Côtes d'Azur

William Turnbull (catalogue), Galeria Freites, Caracas

William Turnbull: New Sculpture (catalogue), Galerie Michael Haas, Berlin

New Beginnings: postwar British art from the collection of Ken Powell (catalogue), Scottish National Gallery of Modern Art, Edinburgh

Bevan, Roger: '"New Displays" at the Tate Gallery makes special rooms for Joseph Beuys and Rebecca Horn', *The Art Newspaper*, no.16, March, p.4

1993 Mellor, David: *The Sixties Art Scene in London* (catalogue), Barbican Art Gallery, London and Phaidon Press, London

1995 Elliott, Patrick: 'William Turnbull', *Galleries Magazine*, November

Packer, William: 'Totemic Images', *The Financial Times*, 21 November

'William Turnbull: Sculpture and paintings', *The News Line*, 21 November, p.7

Kent, Sarah: 'Matter in mind', *Time Out*, 22 November

Benjamin, Marina: 'A twitch away from the straight and narrow', *The Evening Standard*, 30 November, p.31

'Idols from far and near', *Ham and High*, 1 December

Cork, Richard: 'Watchful calm after the storm', *The Times*, 19 December, p.35

Cohen, Bernard: 'William Turnbull: Painter and Sculptor', *Modern Painters*, Winter, pp.30–35 (previously publ. in *Art International*, July/August 1973)

del Renzio, Toni: 'William Turnbull: Serpentine Gallery', *Art Monthly*, no.192, December–January, pp.37–38

Kent, Sarah: 'British Sculpture: A thumbnail sketch', *Here and Now* (exhibition brochure), Serpentine Gallery, London

Robertson, Bryan (intro.): *British Abstract Art Part 2: Sculpture* (catalogue), Flowers East, London

Sylvester, David (intro.): *William Turnbull: sculpture and paintings* (catalogue), Merrell Holberton and Serpentine Gallery, London

Of the Human Form (catalogue), Waddington Galleries, London

Elliott, Ann (intro.): *Sculpture at Goodwood 1*, The Hat Hill Sculpture Foundation, p.64

1996 Abadie, Daniel and Alan Bowness (intro.): *un siècle de sculpture anglaise* (catalogue), galerie nationale du Jeu de Paume, Paris

Capelo, Francisco (intro.): *The Berardo Collection*, Sintra Museum of Modern Art, Portugal

Renfrew, Colin (intro.): *Sculpture in the Close* (catalogue), Jesus College, Cambridge

Hindry, Ann: 'English Sculpture: Playing the Imagination', *Art Press*, no.214, June, pp.20–28 (text in English and French)
The 20th-Century Art Book, Phaidon Press, London
Bonn, Sally: *L'Art en Angleterre 1945–1995*, Nouvelles Éditions Françaises, Paris

1997 Lynton, Norbert (intro.): 'Making Seen the Unseen', *British Contemporary Sculpture 1997/8*, Sculpture at Goodwood
Cowling, Elizabeth: *Surrealism and After: The Gabrielle Keiller Collection* (catalogue), Scottish National Gallery of Modern Art, Edinburgh
Born, Richard A. and Keith Hartley: *From Blast to Pop: Aspects of Modern British Art, 1915–1965*, David and Alfred Smart Museum of Art, University of Chicago

1998 Lambirth, Andrew: 'Age of allusion', *RA Magazine*, Summer, p.21
Packer, William: 'Strength in their simplicity', *The Financial Times*, 30 June, p.18
Coomer, Martin: 'William Turnbull: Waddington', *Time Out*, 8–15 July, p.45
Hilton, Tim: 'Life's all kitsch isn't it?', *The Independent on Sunday*, 16 August
Lynton, Norbert: *British Figurative Art: Part Two: Sculpture* (catalogue), Flowers East, London
Causey, Andrew: *Sculpture Since 1945*, Oxford University Press
Renfrew, Colin (intro.): *William Turnbull: Sculpture and Paintings* (catalogue), Waddington Galleries, London

1999 Taplin, Robert: 'William Turnbull at Barbara Mathes', *Art in America*, February, pp.112–113
Spring, Justin: 'William Turnbull: Barbara Mathes Gallery', *Artforum*, vol.XXXVII, no.6, February, pp.100–101
Russell Taylor, John: 'Around the galleries: Colour Sculptures', *The Times*, 27 October
Robertson, Bryan: 'Colour as Form: British sculpture in the 60s', *Modern Painters*, vol.12, no.4, Winter, pp.30–34

Robertson, Bryan (intro.): *Colour Sculptures: Britain in the sixties* (catalogue), Waddington Galleries, London
Patrizio, Andrew: *Contemporary Sculpture in Scotland*, Craftsman House, Sydney

2000 Thomas, Silke (intro.): *gARTen*, Galerie Thomas, Munich
Collischan, Judy: *Welded Sculpture of the Twentieth Century* (catalogue), Neuberger Museum of Art, Purchase, New York/Lund Humphries, London
Elliott, Ann and Tim Marlow: *Sculpture at Goodwood: British Contemporary Sculpture*, Goodwood

2001 *William Turnbull: Horses – Development of a Theme, Other Sculptures and Paintings* (catalogue), Waddington Galleries, London
Wood, Jon (intro.): *Close Encounters: The Sculptor's Studio in the Age of the Camera* (catalogue), Henry Moore Institute, Leeds
Hyman, James: *The Battle for Realism*, Yale University Press, New Haven and London

2002 Canning, S.E: 'William Turnbull: Sculpture', *The Art Newspaper*, no.126, June, p.4
Harrison, Martin: *Transition, The London Art Scene in the Fifties* (catalogue), Barbican Art Galleries, London
Schmid, Gabriele (intro.): *William Turnbull – Skulpturen* (catalogue), Galerie Thomas, Munich
Meyric Hughes, Henry and Gijs van Tuyl: *Blast to Freeze: British Art in the 20th Century* (catalogue), Kunstmuseum Wolfsburg in association with Hatje Cantz Publishers
Garlake, Margaret (intro.): *Henry Moore and the Geometry of Fear* (catalogue), James Hyman Fine Art, London
United Kingdom United States, (catalogue), Waddington Galleries, London

2003 Renfrew, Colin: 'The Art of Interpretation', *The Scotsman: Scotsman magazine*, 15 March, pp.8–11

2004 *William Turnbull: heads and figures 1953–56* (catalogue), James Hyman Fine Art, London
Stephens, Chris and Katherine Stout (eds.): *Art and the 60s: This Was Tomorrow* (catalogue), Tate Britain, London
The challenge of post-war painting (catalogue), James Hyman Fine Art, London
William Turnbull, Waddington Galleries, London
Paintings, Sculpture and Works on Paper, Waddington Galleries, London
William Turnbull: Paintings 1959–1963, Bronze Sculpture 1954–1958 (catalogue), Waddington Galleries, London

2005 Davidson, Amanda A.: *The Sculpture of William Turnbull*, The Henry Moore Foundation, Hertfordshire in association with Lund Humphries, Hampshire
Lilley, Clare: *William Turnbull Retrospective 1946–2003* (exhibition guide), Yorkshire Sculpture Park, Wakefield
40 Jahre Galerie Thomas, Nr.2, Galerie Thomas, Munich

2006 Bugler, Caroline (ed.): *The Art Fund, 2005 Review*, p. 64

2007 *William Turnbull Sculpture & Paintings from 1946 to 1962* (catalogue), Waddington Galleries, London
Sculpture, Waddington Galleries, London
Agnew, Julian: *Looking Forward: Thirty Contemporary British Artists* (catalogue), Agnew's, London

2008 *Yorkshire Sculpture Park: Landscape for Art*, Yorkshire Sculpture Park, Wakefield

ILLUSTRATED BOOKS

1969 *Basho – The Records of a Weather Exposed Skeleton*, Alistair McAlpine Publishing Ltd., London (limited edition)

1970 *The Garden of Caresses*, translated from the Arabic by Franz Toussaint, drawings by William Turnbull, Alistair McAlpine Publishing Ltd., London (limited edition)

1976 *Der Wassermaler*, by Helmut Heissenbuttel, aquatints by William Turnbull, published by Sybil Albers, Zurich (limited edition)

ARTIST'S STATEMENTS

1956 *This is Tomorrow* (catalogue), Whitechapel Art Gallery, London

1960 'Statements 1949–60', *Uppercase 4*

1961 'The Joining Edge', *Gazette*, No.1

1963 'Images without Temples' (statement and photographs), *Living Arts*, no.1, pp.14–27

1968 'Notes on Sculpture', *Studio International*, vol.176, November, pp.198–201

1969 'Colour in Sculpture', *Studio International*, vol.177, January, p.24

1972 'Liverpool', *Studio International*, July/August, 1991

ACKNOWLEDGMENTS

Waddington Galleries would like to thank
Alex and Johnny Turnbull for their help in
organizing and selecting this exhibition, and
in particular Alex, for allowing us to use the
title of his film *William Turnbull: Beyond Time*
for the title of this exhibition

We would also like to thank Ambassador
Donald Blinken, Tess Jaray, Tim Marlow,
Lord McAlpine of West Green, Sir Nicholas
Serota, Michael Uva and Brian Wall for their
contribution to this catalogue

Above all we would like to thank the artist

WILLIAM TURNBULL BEYOND TIME

9 June – 3 July 2010

Waddington Galleries
11 Cork Street
London
W1S 3LT

Telephone + 44 20 7851 2200
Facsimile + 44 20 7734 4146
mail@waddington-galleries.com
www.waddington-galleries.com

Monday–Friday 10am-6pm
Saturday 10am–1.30pm

We have made every effort to trace the copyright holders of all photographs.
If any individuals have been incorrectly credited, or if there are any omissions, we would be glad to be notified

All Photography by Prudence Cuming Associates, London except for:
cat. no.3: John Well FRPS Photography, Brompton Studio, London
cat. nos. 4 and 26: Jonty Wilde, courtesy Yorkshire Sculpture Park, Wakefield

Designed by www.hoopdesign.co.uk
Printed by www.fandg.co.uk

© William Turnbull, 2010
© Waddington Galleries, London, 2010
All extracts from the film *William Turnbull: Beyond Time* © Alex Turnbull

Published by Waddington Galleries
Co-ordinated by Louise Shorr

ISBN-978-0-9558285-9-1